C000215015

EYEWITNESS
The Rise and Fall of Dorling Kindersley

Christopher Davis

HARRIMAN HOUSE LTD
3A Penns Road
Petersfield
Hampshire
GU32 2EW
GREAT BRITAIN

Tel: +44 (0)1730 233870
Fax: +44 (0)1730 233880
Email: enquiries@harriman-house.com
Website: www.harriman-house.com

First published in Great Britain in 2009

ISBN 978-1-906659-19-6

British Library Cataloguing in Publication Data
A CIP catalogue record for this book can be obtained from the British
Library.

Printed and bound by Butler Tanner & Dennis

Contents

About the Author

Christopher Davis has spent more than 40 years in publishing, the majority of them with DK, which he joined as one of the founding members in 1974. Over the years he graduated from Managing Editor to Editorial Director to Publisher and Deputy Chairman. When Pearson acquired the company in 2000 he was retained as Publisher until his retirement in 2005. He is now a publishing consultant and writer. He lives in London.

Author's Note

This is essentially a personal memoir of the 25 extraordinary years that DK enjoyed as an independent publisher. I set out to capture not just the essence of the company – the pursuit of excellence, the quest for the new, the drive to succeed – but also the shared sense of communal endeavour, and fun, which so many of us enjoyed in the best times at its coalface. It is, of course, just one person's perspective.

I kept no diary (alas) during my three decades with DK so, although this is a work of non-fiction, it relies for the most part on my memory, and therefore any failings of that untrustworthy mechanism are my responsibility.

Nor did I make contemporaneous recordings of conversations. Much of the quoted dialogue, therefore, cannot be read as verbatim duplication, and some of it is self-evidently invented. Likewise, some stories have grown a little taller in the retelling, and some events have been compressed for the sake of brevity or narrative effect. A few characters have been disguised under fictional names. But in all this I have sought to represent an essential truth.

On a personal note, I would have liked to include many more of the individuals who contributed in some significant way to DK's success – they run into the hundreds – but as I approached this task, I realised that the greater the number of names I listed, the more painful the sins of omission would become. To all of you who might feel aggrieved by this decision I offer my apologies.

Naturally, I will be happy to consider any amendments, exclusions and corrections for whenever the revised/condensed/enhanced/mass market/large type/and Folio Society editions of this great work appear.

Christopher Davis, London, 2009.

Bad Night at the Union Hotel

A grisly Frankfurt dawn was battling through the threadbare curtains and seeking purchase on the grimy orange carpet. A barking dog had taken up residence inside my head; my tongue resembled its blanket. As another avalanche of empty bottles cascaded into the belly of the garbage truck in the street below, I was reminded that I had stayed for at least five Rieslings too many in the bar of the Park Hotel, one of the most populated late-night watering hotels during the annual book fair. Publishers, editors, agents, authors, illustrators, photographers, art directors, publicists, production heads, marketeers and sales directors, printers and packagers, patrician elders and arriviste wheeler-dealers, corporate accountants, captains of industry, conmen, cowboys, inveterate dreamers and perpetual no-hopers gathered here or in the slightly more traditional atmosphere of the Frankfurter Hof after their dinner engagements to bray and brag and laugh and leer and, through the misty excesses of their alcoholic intake, reaffirm, to themselves at least, that their place on the great wheel of publishing fortune was secure for another year. Frankfurt was the tipping point, the Oktoberfest of the book world, at which – or so I was led to believe – the future could be staked, won, lost, or merely held at bay. Concepts were pitched, synopses circulated, advances touted, deals bartered, co-editions contracted, promises airily made, and everywhere the cries of 'I'll get back to you' rose to the rafters of the hangar-like halls on thermals of hype.

Alas, I was not waking in the cool Egyptian cotton of the Park Hotel. I was sweating in the skiddy nylon sheets of the Union Hotel, a starless establishment in the impoverished heart of the city's red light district. Across the road was Meier Gustl's Cellar, a once favoured haunt of American GIs, which featured a brass band of portly gents in lederhosen and bogbrush hats whose repetitive oompah oompah boomed through the windows of the hotel until the early hours. If that were not enemy enough of sleep, the curtains were too skimpy to keep out the flashing neon sign of Dr Muller's Sex and Gags Shop, which even now was beaming its on-off technicolour greeting directly into the room. Sex and Gags was a 24-hour business.

I was not alone in the room. The budget of Dorling Kindersley, a newly hatched company, did not run to luxury of any kind. There were only four of us on this initial venture to the book fair in the autumn of 1975: the two founders, Christopher Dorling and Peter Kindersley; Caroline Oakes, who was Christopher's partner and had responsibility for foreign rights; and myself. We had travelled from London in a VW camper van, meandering cross country through the battlefields of northern France, avoiding the autoroutes for as long as possible. We wanted to give ourselves time to recuperate from the midnight-oil madness of the previous weeks when the company's first titles had to be readied for press and a portfolio of future projects prepared for presentation at the fair.

By the time we hit the maelstrom of traffic hurtling down the autobahn into Frankfurt I was accustomed to having Peter Kindersley as my roommate, and to his idiosyncrasies of the night. In one of the puritanical fits of zeal to which he was prone, he had recently decided to forswear alcohol and tobacco, and as a consequence he tended to retire early to bed, at least early by my standards. He was a man with a purpose and a vision. Not for him the booze and loose-tongued banter of the late-night bar crowd; after a soothing herbal tea he enjoyed the untroubled sleep of the virtuous, and neither Meier Gustl's thunderous brass nor Dr Muller's winking neon, nor even the clanking of the all-night trams or the sodden shouts of the city's derelicts, could penetrate his dreams of empire or ruffle the map of his imagined world on which the flag of Dorling Kindersley fluttered from every conquered territory. Total World Domination was his mantra, and though we, his colleagues, may have mocked him for its Führer-like associations, we didn't doubt how seriously he meant it.

Unfortunately for me, the corollary of Peter's early bedtime meant that he would arise refreshed in the hour before dawn, before a sparrow had even contemplated farting, to undertake his yoga and meditation routine. On this particular night I had badly mistimed my return from the bar. Stumbling into the room, after experiencing some difficulty fitting the key into the lock, I tripped in the dark on the edge of the carpet and crashed my knee against the iron frame of the bed onto which I then collapsed with an attack of the hiccups. I was trying to suppress this outbreak when I became aware of the figure on the bed opposite. Peter Kindersley was standing on his head. This so took me aback that I involuntarily released a loud hiccup followed by a sonorous burp.

Jeez, I've blown it now, I thought, when I had recovered sufficient composure to creep across to the basin to brush my teeth. That spells the end of my beautiful career. But when I returned to my bed and slid under the covers, Peter was still impassively motionless in his yogic position (Frog Greeting the Dawn). Maybe, I wondered, he's in such a trance-like state that he wasn't even aware of my chaotic return. On which optimistic note, I fell asleep.

A few minutes later, the telephone rang.

'Bloody hell,' I muttered, sitting bolt upright in bed. 'Who can that be?'

Peter didn't move. He was now in a different position (Heron Bending in the Wind). I reached over and picked up the receiver. There was a distant cacophony of voices and clinking glasses. Then a throaty, 40-a-day American voice was wheedling in my ear.

'Hey, honey, why d'ya disappear? Come on out and play…'

Oh God, I thought, this is turning into a night I want to

forget. But how do you forget what you can't remember?

The fog of my sojourn in the bar was beginning to clear. This had to be someone I will call Marcy Buttbaum, a generously proportioned rights director from one of New York's publishing behemoths, celebrated for her appetite for younger males, an appetite that seemed to increase at every passing book fair as she sensed the onset of her sell-by date. I remembered that the crush in the bar had resulted in our being wedged into a corner where she had taken advantage of the situation to thrust her deeply tanned cleavage under my nose. I had needed an escape route, almost impossible in that crowded space until the moment came when Marcy turned to accept a light from the barman. I had slid off my bar stool and hurried back to the hotel.

Evidently she was not to be denied.

'What are you doing, honey?'

'Doing? I was trying to sleep.'

'Sleep?' she shouted. 'Who needs sleep at Frankfurt?'

'Shh!' I said, as quietly and urgently as possible.

'Why shh? Is there somebody else there?'

'Er, yes, there is as a matter of fact.'

'Well, I must say,' said Marcy in a frosty voice, 'if I'd known you had someone all snuggled up waiting for you…'

'No, no, you don't understand. It's not like that at all, not that kind of relationship,' I said.

'Whadd'ya mean? You pick up a hooker on the way back?'

'No, for God's sake. I'm sharing a room with a colleague. A male colleague.'

I looked apprehensively over at Peter's bed. He was still gazing impassively at the wall ahead, though he had slipped into another position (Snow Falling on Monkeys). His big toe was hovering close to the light switch.

'A man! Oh my God! I might have known it. You're just another of those typical British public school products, weaned on whadd'ya call it – spotted dick and sodomy. You all grow up to be wankers or spankers, usually both. Keep your uptight little ass polished for your friend.'

'Marcy, for Christ's sake, it's my boss.'

'Better yet, kid, you'll make it all the way to the top once he's made it to your bottom.'

'No, no, no. We're a new company. We don't have the budget for single rooms…'

But Marcy had rung off, to prowl for more submissive meat in the Frankfurt reserve.

Now I had opened one eye, after a brief and fitful sleep, to be confronted by the ghastliness of the room and the embarrassments of the night. I wondered if Peter would mention the disturbances I had caused. I wondered, again, if he had even noticed. I decided to wait it out before mentioning anything or offering an apology. These ruminations were interrupted, however, by a sudden burst of feverish activity across the room. Peter was striding round the perimeter walls in his pyjamas, stamping furiously with his bare feet.

'Cockroaches!' he roared. 'Legions of them! Bastards! Kill, kill, kill!'

After some minutes spent slaughtering the invertebrates, Peter decided to take a shower to remove the carcases from the soles of his feet. Unfortunately, the Union Hotel's idea of an ensuite bathroom was a basin against the wall and a shower placed like a telephone booth in the middle of the bedroom. The latter was, predictably, imperfectly sealed, so that as he doused his feet under the steaming jet, spouts of water sprayed from the top corners of the cubicle to form four puddles on the grimy orange carpet in which I could see, in the flashes of neon light, the enfeebled waving of a host of cockroach legs.

Waving but not drowning, I thought. I wonder if I can say the same of myself. Or the company. Will Dorling Kindersley need to be as indestructible as a cockroach to survive its first Frankfurt Book Fair?

Christopher Davis and Christopher Dorling loading the Kindersley camper van that transported us to Frankfurt for several years.

Spreads on the Bed

As I eased myself out of bed and picked my way through the insect carnage to the washbasin, I felt the disinclination of my limbs to obey instructions. It was like taking a reluctant dog on a walk. It wasn't just the self-inflicted excesses of the Frankfurt nightlife that had wiped me out; it was the cumulative effect of the past nine months when I, like everyone else at our tiny fledgling enterprise, had worked round the clock to establish the company. We had faced numerous obstacles, but we had made it, by a whisker. The finished books were now in place, ready to be unveiled. The rest of the staff back home could take a few days off to recuperate, but the four of us in Germany faced a gruelling five days of wall-to-wall meetings – presenting, persuading, negotiating, and, most wearying of all, walking the floors of the huge halls in search of new customers.

Frankfurt is not the healthiest place at the best of times. In October, when the autumn mists rise from the river and mingle with the traffic fumes and the gritty output of the industrial smokestacks, it seems to be transformed into the European Centre for Snotty Diseases. The influx of thousands of publishing folk from all corners of the globe into the unventilated halls rapidly promotes the spread of some debilitating virus, so that it becomes commonplace for meetings to be punctuated by eruptions of sneezing, snuffling and expectorating. Those suffering from Frankfurt Flu are not comforted by having to wait in long lines, usually in the rain, for one of the city's taxis. If you have a dinner date only ten minutes away by cab it is wise to set out an hour ahead. In fact, you have to stand in line for everything – ten or fifteen minutes for a beer or a Sekt, then five or ten minutes to get a stall in the loo. And in those days (it has improved somewhat since) the food available on the concession stands would never have found its way onto a health guru's menu – rolls of white bread stolidly filled with sausage, ham or cheese and, least appetising of all, a bowl of greenish broth in which a knackwurst lurked like a crocodile, commonly referred to as Turdensuppe. For those in need of fibre and essential vitamins, the Frankfurt Book Fair was a wasteland.

Before venturing out into that wasteland, however, we had to convert the hotel bedroom into a semi-civilised space. No easy task. With the telephone kiosk shower in the middle and the sodden carpet around it, it would always resemble a condemned refugee centre. But, in 1975, the funds did not extend to renting a stand at the fair itself. This grotty room had to serve as the showplace for our first printed titles and the dummy presentations of forthcoming projects which

Peter was already laying out on his hastily made bed. He and Christopher planned to meet with the major customers here while Caroline and I would venture into the fair and round up others to make the pilgrimage to this mangy hostelry.

'Now listen,' he was saying as I struggled to pull on my trousers without falling over, 'your job with Caroline is to target the Americans in Hall 5 and persuade them to come down here. I'll give you the list of names. The big chiefs are usually gone after a couple of days so you've got to hit them early. Got it?'

'Yeah, sure.'

'And once you've ticked off all the Americans, I want you to tackle the major European markets. You won't get them to come here. But you need to take a spare set of materials with you and see if you can make a breakthrough into at least one of the big publishers in each country. You'll have to do a lot of foot-slogging, so I hope you've got the energy.'

He gave me an old-fashioned look as if to remind me that my nocturnal activities would have to be kept in check. I busied myself with my tie.

As I closed the bedroom door behind me, I ingested the charms of the Union Hotel. No carpet softened the slate-grey floors of the corridors, no pictures brightened the walls. A few low-wattage bulbs shed a spectral light onto the piles of dirty linen outside each room, while the air thrummed with the lingering afterburn of the morning's ablutions. How could we possibly persuade the presidents and vice-presidents of the great Manhattan empires to leave their comfortable shag pile and venture, chequebook in hand, into this remnant of the Stalags?

Peter Kindersley was unfazed by this. So confident was he in the strength of his own ideas, he deemed it would be the Americans' loss not to make the journey.

'Don't take no for an answer,' he had said, jabbing at my chest with his finger. 'They know they might miss out on something if they don't come. We have let the key players know that we wouldn't have left Mitchell Beazley and started a new company unless we had some special projects up our sleeves.'

In this he was right. MB was only six years old by this time yet its reputation in publishing circles was fairly substantial. James Mitchell and John Beazley had left Nelson in the late '60s to launch their company, and taken two other colleagues with them – Peter Kindersley as art director, and Christopher Dorling, by training a cartographer, to assist James with sales. While Mitchell was the vibrant, charismatic character at the forefront of the company, Beazley worked quietly in the background on production and in making contacts in the city. The genius in MB's early books, however, lay in the revolutionary art direction, in which Peter played a conspicuous part. There was a complexity on the page that hadn't previously been seen in illustrated reference books – more expensive to produce for sure, but the company proved that these costs could be offset by pre-selling co-editions to multiple markets around the world. James Mitchell was masterly at the latter, employing a technique that combined charm and ruthlessness in equal measure. A foreign publisher would enter the sumptuous suite at the Park Hotel in Frankfurt where MB displayed their wares, and before he realised what was happening, would find that one of his hands was clasping a flute of champagne while the other was twisted up behind his back as he was "persuaded" to accept an outrageous deal.

MB created several landmark books in those first years including Hugh Johnson's *World Atlas of Wine* and *The* (mould-breaking) *Joy of Sex*. But the relationship between the founding quartet soured when Mitchell and Beazley promised Dorling and Kindersley shares and then abruptly withdrew the offer before selling off a slice of the company to VNU in Holland. Thereafter Christopher and Peter were always looking for an exit. It came in the summer of '74 – they left separately, but it was no surprise to hear that they had subsequently teamed up and had visited Frankfurt that year "undercover" to test out a few ideas. They needed to be covert because James Mitchell was unforgiving to anyone who left his employ for a competitor. The prospect of Peter and Christopher setting up a rival venture set his adrenaline in motion, and for years afterwards we at DK found ourselves at the wrong end of his attempts to discredit us, both with customers and with the press.

He failed. And he failed principally because the book ideas with which DK was able to arm itself were by and large strong enough to withstand his assault. For years Peter had tried to persuade Mitchell to produce a really practical guide to photography. This was the burgeoning age of the SLR camera, and nothing existed on the bookshelves for the consumer apart from the rather arid, sparsely illustrated, semi-academic tomes published by Focal Press. James just couldn't see the market for a more populist approach.

Fortunately for us, the rest of the world could. *The Book of Photography* by John Hedgecoe was the ace in our pack that Frankfurt, the trump card in our dogged efforts to gain an entrée into the European markets. Caroline and I walked onto the stands of the major houses like mendicants; they didn't know who we were, and they'd never heard of Dorling Kindersley.

'Nous sommes un packageur nouveau,' I stammered to the publisher at Larousse, who eyed me suspiciously as I attempted to disencumber myself from the art bags that hung from my shoulders like panniers on a donkey. But as soon as we opened the bags and produced the dummy spreads, the implicit disdain in his demeanour morphed into surprise, surprise into curiosity, and then into admiration. He wanted to do business. After several such encounters, we knew we had a global winner.

It is probable that what impressed these publishers more was the evidence that we were not just one-trick ponies; there were other projects in the portfolio that caught the eye. These were not anonymous "packaged" books; they were properly authored works of reference, created according to the principles laid down by Peter and Christopher at the outset – namely, to build a backlist with authoritative names and to ensure that every title was produced to the highest standards of design to give it a cutting edge over the competition.

At the end of the week we drove away down the autobahn in exhausted triumph. We had enticed enough big American publishers to brave the hinterland of the Union Hotel to secure orders on the key titles, and the many miles that Caroline and I had covered as we targeted the French, German, Dutch, Italian, Spanish, Scandinavian and Japanese stands had been rewarded not only with a sackful of business cards but also enough genuine interest that could be followed up and converted into sales. At the same time, there was no denying that Frankfurt had done us in. Sleepless nights in the hotel, plus stress, bad diet, streaming colds, stomach flu and, in my case at least, toxic quantities of alcohol and cigarettes, had rendered us almost catatonic. The kilometres on the autobahn slipped by in a haze. We peeled off in the early evening and trundled into Luxembourg where we found a haven in a rural inn with a welcoming fire and a simple warming supper of freshly caught trout. We slept like dogs beneath voluminous duvets, puffed up to envelop one like clumps of towering cumuli.

For myself, sleep did not entirely knit up the ravelled sleeve of care. In the morning I woke to find the pillowcase coated in clusters of ringlets, not from some phantom maiden in my dreams but, shockingly, from my own head. Aghast, I stood in the shower and watched the water struggling to escape through what looked like a beaver dam of pubic hair around the plughole. Was this payback time, I wondered, for my impulsive gesture in July when, after watching Arthur Ashe, the epitome of cool, demolish Jimmy Connors, the epitome of brash, in the Wimbledon final, I had dashed to my local Fulham hairdresser and demanded a styling to match my hero's? Now my Afro was blocking a drain in Luxembourg. I'll never know the cause for sure, there was no satisfactory diagnosis when I returned home, and in any event my locks

were fully restored a few months later. But one thing is certain
– mentally, physically, emotionally, Frankfurt 1975 was the
most punishing experience. The subsequent upside was that it
hardened all of us to face whatever slings outrageous fortune
might hurl in our direction.

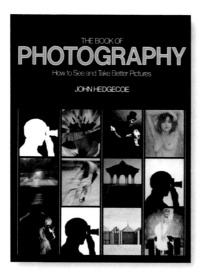

Of the first crop of DK titles, John Hedgecoe's book was the star performer.
It became a million-seller.

Mistress of Wine

It had been a hard decision for me to leave Mitchell Beazley to join the embryonic Dorling Kindersley. The former was well established and brimming with expansionist conceits. Among other things the company was about to embark on *The Joy of Knowledge*, a hugely ambitious multi-volume encyclopedia. On a personal level I felt reasonably optimistic about my chances of progressing within the editorial hierarchy. And besides, the winter of 1974 was one of deep national discontent, an unpropitious time to start a new publishing venture. It would mean transferring from an ocean liner to a sailing dinghy in very troubled economic waters.

On the other hand, Christopher and Peter had initially hired me to join MB, and it was with them that I had worked for two years rather than with James Mitchell. And, although I had been counselled by others that putting your faith in Peter Kindersley was akin to putting your head into a lion's cage, my gut instinct was to ignore this. For some reason I did trust him. And there was one crucial factor in his favour: he was a man with a powerful creative and commercial instinct for new publishing ideas. As I mulled over the dilemma of whether to stay or go, it came to me that, apart from James's new obsession – *The Joy of Knowledge* – the breakthrough concepts at MB had grown rather thin on the vine recently, and there was a certain complacency in the fact that they were falling back on repetitive formulae. What Dorling and Kindersley were offering was both new and refreshingly different. In the end, that clinched it. Follow the vision.

There were a couple of immediate downsides to swallow – a drop in salary and a change of location. Of the two, the latter was the more unpalatable. One of the incidental pleasures of being at Mitchell Beazley in the early '70s was its location in the heart of Soho. The offices were a buzzy place to work, the company was inclined to throw parties at the drop of a hat, my colleagues were highly congenial, and the semi-bohemian raffishness of the area's bars, clubs and eateries was a source of constant stimulus to those imbued with the cheerful hedonism of the time. Now Peter was telling me that the headquarters of the new company were located in the back bedroom of his South London home, a terraced house in an unremarkable street miles away from the sybaritic watering holes to which I was accustomed. It might have been Outer Mongolia as far as I was concerned.

On a freezing morning in late December 1974 I made the trek from my house in Fulham to SE11 for my first working day in the employ of Dorling Kindersley. The company had temporarily relocated from the back bedroom to a studio belonging to Peter's brother, Richard, a few streets away. There were ten of us in all. In addition to the two principals, Caroline and myself, there were three other escapees from MB – Roger Bristow, Jackie Douglas and Sheilagh Noble – while Bridget Morley had been hired from Reader's Digest. Linda Nash had already been working for some months as a designer on the first projects, and there was an editor from the West Country in place who was reputed to have specialist knowledge of photography but who seemed to be in a semi-permanent state of disrepair from fights with his ex-wife's boyfriend. He didn't last long and in his place we took on David Reynolds from Time-Life. Over the next few months various freelancers were added to the mix so that soon there was a struggle for desk space, the kettle, the copying machine and the solitary loo.

Outside the Kennington studio, 1975. Back row, from left: Roger Bristow, Derek Ungless, Bridget Morley, Sheilagh Noble, David Reynolds, Peter Kindersley. Front row, from left: Jackie Douglas, Christopher Dorling, Caroline Oakes, Christopher Davis.

Kennington in those days was a culinary desert. Our choices at lunchtime lay between a dismal hostelry that served what we called Tortoise Pie and Chips, a suspiciously empty curry house, and a Greek Cypriot establishment whose reheated moussaka was reckoned to teem with enough salmonella to poleaxe a horse. It therefore suited me very well that one of the first titles on the list, *The Taste of Wine*, allowed me to spend a good deal of time away from Kennington with the author.

Pamela Vandyke Price MW was a formidable lady who lived alone in a battered high-ceilinged flat on the first floor of a South Kensington terrace. She had decided that I, as well as being her editor, was, with my limited expertise in the subject, the perfect model for the intended readership of her book, and she would therefore experiment on me as if I were a pupil in the master class she was about to give. She would blind-test me on wines and elicit my untutored opinions.

Two mornings a week at 10 o'clock I would ring the bell of Pamela's flat, climb the gloomy staircase and wait for her to open the door. This sometimes took several minutes as she had to manoeuvre the line of empty bottles which stretched back from her front door along one side of the hall passage, round the living room, and then back along the other side of the hall and into her kitchen. If the front door was opened too quickly and knocked over the first bottle in the line, it set in motion a disastrous domino effect. The first time this happened it created such a racket that the ancient occupant of the flat above emerged in an alarmed state onto the landing, while at the same time the resident of the flat below was thumping angrily on the ceiling with a broom.

Pamela was in a fluster; she hated untoward disruptions of her daily routine. I did my best to calm her while crawling round her apartment to retrieve the bottles that were rolling hither and thither across the uneven floorboards. The problem was compounded by the discovery that not all the bottles were empty. She was in the habit of collecting the dregs to create, over time, a culture of vinegar. Thus there were several bottles in various stages of maturation toward the culture she called "Mother", a large and slippery tongue of frothy substance. Now I saw to my horror that one of the "Mothers" had escaped from its upturned bottle and was slithering across the kitchen floor.

'Oh, prudent be!' shrieked Pamela. 'That's taken months to grow. There's nothing for it but to chuck it.' At which point she scooped up "Mother" in a dustpan and dropped it in the sink where it slipped down the plughole like an eel under a rock.

After this episode I was extremely circumspect on my visits to the flat, carefully keeping to the centre of the hallway for fear of disturbing even one soldier in the ranks of the bottle army.

Once settled in the living room, Pamela would offer coffee and we would spend the next hour discussing the structure of the book, how she was progressing with a particular section, and the delivery schedule. Sometimes Bridget Morley, in her capacity as art director on the title, was there too to elicit Pamela's views on the design of the book and to talk through the practical details of illustrating her text. There was no clock in the room and Pamela didn't wear a wristwatch, but she seemed to have an unerring goose-like gift for knowing when the magic hour of eleven had struck.

'Now,' she would say, parking her manuscript on the side table, 'time to turn our attention to the grape.'

And with that she would stride off to extract a bottle of white from the fridge. Concealing the label from my vision, she would uncork the bottle and pour a slug into a couple of glasses. I recalled the section she had recently submitted on how to judge a wine by its colour and its nose before tasting it; she had been particularly severe on the subject of having clean glasses to hand to be able to judge the former properly.

'Hold your glass up to the light, dear, and tell me what you see.'

What I saw and what I said I could see were rather different. The particular glass I held up was mottled with heavy thumbprints and its rim edged with smears of lipstick. Furthermore, Pamela's windows looked as if they hadn't been cleaned since VE Day, and against the dismal backdrop of the February sky it was almost impossible to detect any quality of light or colour in the wine. It could have been pee, for all I knew.

'Maybe it has a slightly straw-like colour,' I hedged.

'Tip-top!' clapped Pamela. 'Oh, I can see you're going to be a very promising pupil. Now swirl the wine round in the glass, sniff deeply, and tell me what scents it conjures up. It could be cinnamon, it could be almonds, it could be citrus, it could find an echo in innumerable associations from your memory bank of smells. It's vital to be honest and spontaneous in your tasting notes when you first encounter a wine.'

I buried my nose in the glass. My honest, spontaneous reaction was that it reminded me of the family labrador's blanket with overtones of Pamela's lipstick.

'A hint of stable perhaps?' I offered tentatively.

'Sable, did you say?' squawked Pamela. 'Oh, how wonderful! I'd never thought of that, but now you mention it...'

'No, sorry, I said stable. I thought it was a natural association with the straw colouring.'

'Hmm, I'm not so sure about that,' said Pamela, taking another sniff, 'but let's see about the taste.'

I took a gulp and swilled it around my molars. Yuck. The wine had a cloying edge to it. Not what I wanted at eleven in the morning on a nearly empty stomach.

'Well?' enquired Pamela.

'I'm not sure,' I replied. 'Maybe it will grow on me.'

'Have a drop more,' said Pamela, refilling my glass, 'and let's see if it does.'

I stoutly tried to find virtues in the bottle but for the moment they escaped me. I felt I might appreciate it better with food, or even after food, an opinion with which Pamela concurred.

'It's from the Jura,' she said. 'The straw colour is a giveaway. Now let's try something else.'

And so the ritual was repeated, but fortunately for me the next bottle was a bone dry white with a flinty crispness to it.

'Now, Christopher dear, do you think this was grown on a north or south-facing slope?'

'South?' I guessed.

'Absolutely right. How did you know? And was it grown in chalk or clay soil?'

'Chalk?'

Again I was right.

'But do you like it?' asked Pamela. 'That's the key question.'

'Yes, I do. Very much.'

'Excellent. Let's finish the bottle and then you must go.'

And so it was that, twice a week, towards the end of the morning, I would stumble out into Queen's Gate, starving hungry, bemused, half-cut, my head reeling with the myriad associations Pamela had summoned up in her increasingly fanciful attempts to define the characteristics of the wines we sampled.

'Do you detect saddle soap in this one, dear?' was a typically far-fetched example.

No, I was tempted to reply, but I can detect the backside that last sat on it.

Usually I was carrying Pamela's latest chapter under my arm, which she insisted had to be edited and couriered back to her hairdresser by the following afternoon, when she would read it while under the dryer. By the time I got back to my desk I was in no state to bring careful consideration to her prose, which, apart from being chaotically organised, was written in a breathless style that badly needed doctoring. I would have to tackle it that night if I had sobered up enough; if not, it would mean facing up to it in the cold light of dawn. Either way I knew it would do my head in, trying to turn her manuscript into a text fit for a reference book.

I will, however, always remain indebted to Pamela Vandyke Price. She taught me the value of honesty in wine appreciation, to ignore reputation and received wisdom while simply learning to distinguish which styles of wine one really liked. Her influence opened up to me a whole new world of tasting pleasures.

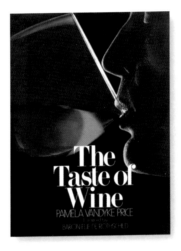

Books on wine were a growing trend in the 1970s, but the sales of Pamela Vandyke Price's title didn't scale the heights we were expecting.

Ashes and Diamonds

Aside from *The Taste of Wine*, there were two other books being worked on during those first months in the Kennington studio – the aforementioned *Book of Photography* by John Hedgecoe, and *The Origin of Johnny*. All three were moving ahead well in terms of their design, but the same could not be said of the texts. John Hedgecoe's photographs were ideal for demonstrating to amateurs how to raise their skills to a more professional level but, although he knew what he wanted to say about technique, composition and so forth, he was frustratingly unable to articulate it on paper. In the end we were obliged to hire Adrian Bailey as an amanuensis to work with him, but by then the schedule on the book was way off track. We had been hoping that, like the other two projects, it would be delivered in time for Christmas 1975.

The Origin of Johnny suffered from different but equally threatening convulsions. Nigel Calder, the author originally contracted, had delivered a manuscript which Peter Kindersley claimed was unacceptable. He was sacked. In his place Malcolm Ross Macdonald took up the challenge, starting again from scratch. It was a tough call to get the tone and level right, explaining the story of evolution from the Big Bang to the here-and-now of a young boy, and even tougher when working against a much shortened deadline.

Then, one morning in the summer, everything was thrown out of whack. A phone call came through from John Marshall, the UK representative of the Dutch printers, Van Leer, with whom all three titles had been placed. Peter and Christopher took the call, then disappeared outside for some time. When they returned to the studio, they asked us to gather round.

Christopher spoke.

'I'm sorry to say that we've got some rather bad news to report. We have just heard that Van Leer's reproduction house in Amsterdam was completely destroyed by fire last night.'

A terrible silence filled the room. We all knew at once what that meant. The illustrations and photographs for our first three books were being reproduced at this plant and as we were by then well advanced into the production schedules, a high proportion of each title's images would have been in Amsterdam. It threatened the very existence of the company.

'Completely destroyed, did you say?' someone asked. 'Nothing at all to be salvaged?'

'Totally burnt out. It was an old building with an arched gateway that proved too narrow for the fire trucks to get through. All that remains is a heap of twisted, charred machinery.'

'That does it,' said Peter. 'We'll never get these titles out on time. Might as well close down the company and start again.'

Surprisingly for someone who was usually the most positive and determined of the group, he seemed to be the most defeated by this disaster. For a while, the rest of us were too numb to speak. But then a spirit of defiance began to creep in. Maybe it was possible to duplicate what we had lost. Why should we all have worked such punishing hours to be thwarted by this random Act of God?

'You know, I really think we shouldn't give up,' I said. 'We haven't lost everything. It just seems like it right now. It's time that is against us more than anything, finding replacement pictures in short order, re-commissioning artworks, and getting them reproduced…'

'I'm sure we can enlist the support of the photographers, illustrators and picture agencies,' said Bridget. 'They wouldn't want to see a promising young company go under.'

Gradually everyone warmed to the challenge, and chipped in with practical suggestions. All except Peter. He seemed to feel that the world had conspired against him, that it was all over with his bright new venture.

'Somebody show some initiative,' he said. 'What we need is a drink.'

Hours later we were mostly legless. Collective despair had been replaced by collective determination, until finally we were banded together in a mush of sentimental togetherness. Juliet Kindersley had helped Peter home. I followed shortly afterwards. He was conked out in a chair.

'Oh dear,' wailed Juliet. 'Do you think that's the end of

everything? It would be heart-breaking.'

'No, it's not the end,' I said. 'Peter may not realise it yet but the rest of us have decided we are going to rescue the situation. We've all made a commitment to this company and we are damned if we are going to let all the work we have put in for the past six months go to waste. So tell him, when he wakes up, that the fat lady hasn't even arrived at the theatre yet...'

Memory has erased most of that summer of 1975. It is a blur of long hours and late nights. Page by page we replaced or re-commissioned the images lost in the fire. The support we had from artists, photographers, picture researchers and their agencies was simply tremendous. Gradually the shrinking schedules were clawed back. There was still a chance of delivering two titles for autumn publication, though not *The Book of Photography*.

In the midst of this recovery period we somehow moved the company from Kennington to King Street in Covent Garden, where space was opening up after the market's relocation to Nine Elms. At least it was a step closer to civilisation, although in those uncertain days when the whole area was threatened with demolition and redevelopment, there was only one wine bar. Later, when the Piazza had been saved from destruction, they sprouted like mushrooms as the lofts and warehouses filled up with all kinds of creative enterprises. That was our first slice of overdue good luck – to land in a part of London that would become one of the most attractive places to work in the whole city and which we would inhabit for the next quarter of a century.

Recovering the lost ground on the fire-damaged books was a formidable task. At the same time we had to invent new projects for the following year and therefore prepare presentations to raise funding at the upcoming Frankfurt.

In those days books on the subject of the ancient world and the early civilisations were perennial bankers. Peter Kindersley had been determined to uncover a new angle on these topics, and in Jacquetta Hawkes had found an eminent archaeologist who had always wanted to write a book revealing, as she described it, 'what was happening at the same time as what'. Her aim was to discuss whether new civilising developments in technology, culture and society in different parts of the world were spontaneous or whether they occurred as a result of contact or influence spreading from elsewhere. She was grateful for the opportunity to develop this idea in a graphically illustrated volume, though Michael Sissons, her agent, was extremely reluctant at first to entrust one of his prize authors to work with an unproven packaging outfit.

Jacquetta Hawkes and J.B. Priestley lived in a handsome period house on the edges of Stratford-upon-Avon. It had previously been occupied by Sir Bernard and Lady Docker who, in the 1950s and '60s, had been a byword for vulgarity among the über-rich. The hallmark of their taste became clear soon after we arrived for lunch and were ushered into the book-lined study where J.B. Priestley stood mournfully puffing on his pipe.

'What'll you have to drink?' he enquired without much enthusiasm, and then opened a panel to reveal a cocktail cabinet concealed behind the fake books.

'I don't think them Dockers were what you might call lovers of literature,' he growled in his lugubrious Yorkshire voice.

Lunch was a somewhat stilted affair. We tried to make use of our time with Jacquetta to reach an accord on the structure and schedule of the book while simultaneously struggling not to be distracted by the sight and sound of J.B. Priestley slurping his soup, which, at every quivering spoonful, threatened to douse his yellow tie. As he only wore yellow ties, I imagined he must have a whole rail of them in his wardrobe, each one decorated with variegated patterns of soup stains.

'What shall we wear today, sir?' enquires the loyal manservant. 'Will it be the Vichyssoise, the Minestrone, or the Split Pea? Or perhaps the French Onion will go well with your brown tweed jacket?'

Jacquetta by contrast was rather stiff and formal. Not many jokes there. Some years later, having read her account of her courtship with Priestley, I tried to imagine the pair of them having sex in a box at the theatre and wished I had known of those encounters when we met them. Priestley didn't seem to have a lot of fun left in him, and had retreated into grumpy generalisations about all the 'clever, dull young men' working in the arts in London. We came away feeling that he might have been tarring us with the same brush.

Our next trip in search of an author could not have been more different. I had mooted the idea that we should create a practical illustrated guide for all those wannabes who were dreaming of the good life – baking their own bread, brewing their own beer, raising their own livestock on a smallholding, etc. Peter said at once that there was only one man for that – John Seymour, who had already written two engaging narratives on living off the land in Suffolk. We discovered that he had moved to a 60-acre Welsh farm near Cardigan, and made arrangements to visit him. We decided to make a mini-break out of the trip. Linda, my wife, came along, as did Juliet Kindersley and some of her menagerie of animals, including a couple of dachshunds, a cat, and a tortoise lodged on the rear window shelf of the car which crapped down the back of my neck. This didn't ease the discomfort I was already feeling from having smashed my coccyx – a foolish episode in which I had sailed down a children's slide in the dark after a bibulous dinner party and flattened my arse on the sun-baked ground. I was now obliged to sit on a rubber ring at my desk and then here in the back of this overcrowded Ford Granada. Peter Kindersley was not a relaxing driver, a risky mix of aggression and inattention, and his erratic cornering when we reached the winding roads of West Wales threw me around on my ring like a wrecked sailor on a life raft.

Our spirits, however, were high. The countryside was bathed in late summer sun and we were looking forward to sampling the delights of the self-sufficient table which John had so vividly summoned up in his books – slabs of home-smoked ham, hunks of home-baked bread with cheese, tomatoes fresh off the vine, and a couple of pints of home-brewed ale.

Alas, when dreams become reality... As we drove into the farm a slanting rain began to fall, mottling the nettles which grew in profusion around the perimeter of the yard. The place was suffused with an air of dankness and neglect. Broken machinery rusted in one corner, the slates on the roof of the barn were cracked or missing, the paint on the front door was peeling. There was no sign of John Seymour. There was no sign of anyone, and nobody answered the doorbell.

We decided to explore round the back of the house and what we found was dismaying. The place looked derelict, quite unlike the beautiful woodcuts with which John's books had been illustrated (by Sally, his former wife) and which had conjured up an idyllic vision of rural plenitude. There didn't seem to be any livestock around either. The farm appeared to have been abandoned.

'Are you sure we have come to the right place?' said Peter, somewhat impatiently.

'I'm afraid so,' I replied. 'The farm's name was carved into the gate.'

At that moment we spotted a thin stream of smoke coming from behind a haystack. Following it to its source we stumbled upon three rain-soaked hippies lying at its base where they were morosely sharing a joint.

'Excuse me,' said Peter. 'Can you tell us where we might find John Seymour?'

'Over there, man,' replied one. 'In the caravan.'

In the far corner of the field where it dipped down close to the river was an ancient post-war model. Peter strode off purposefully towards it followed by Linda and myself, while Juliet, the dachshunds and the cat cautiously picked their way through the cowpats. As we came closer to the caravan it became apparent that it was rocking back and forth. A rhythmic squeaking emanated from its rusty springs.

It was obvious that John was Otherwise Engaged, but Peter seemed impervious to this possibility. He had driven 250 miles to track down his quarry and he wasn't going to wait a minute longer. He thumped on the door. The rocking continued. He thumped again, even harder, and shouted. Silence. The rocking stopped and the springs settled back with a sigh. After a minute or two there was a clumping of boots inside and the door opened to reveal John Seymour in a state of cheerful dishevelment. He was a large man in his mid-sixties with an amused weather-beaten face framed by bushy ginger sideburns. His check shirt was unbuttoned and only partially tucked into a pair of muddy moleskin trousers, which he was now securing at the waist with an old striped tie.

'Ah, gentlemen, good afternoon!' he boomed. 'You know, the harder you prune a rose, the more it blooms. I find that applies to myself. The older I get, the more vigorous my urges. Raging against the dying of the light, I dare say.'

He clambered down the steps and shook our hands. He was followed by a dark, shapely woman. John introduced her.

'We have to live in this caravan because the house is full up,' he said. 'You see, when my wife walked out, I advertised for volunteers to learn the arts of self-sufficiency. Must have had a thousand replies, but I couldn't cope with sifting through them so I just took the first seven that I opened. Probably a mistake. Half of them can't even dig a hole in the ground.'

'Yes, we saw some of them,' said Peter. 'They weren't exactly looking productive.'

'Well, how about some lunch?' enquired John. 'I don't have much in the caravan, I'm afraid.'

I had already suspected as much. Peering through the window I had glimpsed a loaf of sliced white bread, proprietary supermarket brands of butter and cheese, and a few cans of beer. Nothing that reflected the harvest of a self-sufficient life.

'Let's go to Elsie's down the road,' said John. 'She runs a pub out of her front room.'

'This could be a disaster,' said Peter grimly as we followed John in the car. 'He seems to have abandoned self-sufficiency altogether. I don't see how we can get the book we need out of him.'

But Elsie's tiny hostelry lifted us out of our gloom. After a ploughman's lunch and a couple of pints of 'thin, warm, flat, Welsh, bitter beer', John warmed to the themes of the book idea and was certainly cheered by our prognosis of its potential in other markets of the world (money, or the lack of it, was the perennial bugbear of his life). And, whatever the state of his wifeless farm and the ineffectual labours of his listless band of hippies, he still talked vigorously and optimistically of what could and should be done.

'Britain can feed itself. I'm convinced of it. All we have to do is persuade the government to go back to an orderly system of crop rotation and boycott the self-interested groups who promote agribusiness and the wholesale use of pesticides and, in so doing, destroy both the natural life of the countryside and the human livelihoods of rural communities.'

I was impressed. I was finding John Seymour both persuasive

and engaging. And there was something endearing about his hopeless management of his own affairs when contrasted with his practical vision of the future of farming.

'And if we can communicate that on a small scale,' he continued, 'teaching people the elements of self-sufficiency even if they only have a tiny plot of land at their disposal, then we may build up a community of converts who recognise that what is home-grown and home-made tastes better and is better for you and we might just engender a revolution in this once green and pleasant land.'

By the time we left Elsie's parlour we were all in agreement about how to proceed with the book. The farm was too ramshackle to photograph as a setting but we could send a photographer to capture the techniques of husbandry, following John through the seasons, from sowing the grain to reaping the harvest to baking the bread and so forth. Then, using these pictures as reference, we would create through illustrations an idealised, almost picture-book world in which the dreaming reader could see only sunlight falling on stooks and ne'er a glimpse of rain falling on banks of nettles. From a summer tarnished by ashes, I felt we had unearthed a diamond.

I was sufficiently buoyed by the outcome that on the return journey I barely noticed the irregularities of Peter's driving or the discomforts of my coccyx. Nor did I mind particularly that the tortoise had once more crapped down the back of my sweater. This book could give us lift-off, I mused. It will have the charm and vigour of John's personality but, more than that, it will touch a common pulse

The Godfathers of East 50th Street

So we returned from that challenging Frankfurt Book Fair of 1975, physically and mentally battered but with promises under our belt. Now the embryonic ideas had to be converted into real books. Jacquetta Hawkes was not a problem – her chapters, written in an elegant mandarin style, were delivered with reassuring regularity, and she was supported by a fellow archaeologist in the research for the maps we created. John Seymour, however, lived a life of companionable disorder, easily distracted by offers to go fishing or by extended afternoons in Elsie's front parlour. Besides which, he was struggling to make the farm productive with the supine help of the hippy apprentices.

But it was easy to forgive him his erratic adherence to delivery dates because when a chapter did arrive, it was impossible not to be charmed. It might be lighter on the practical specifics than we needed, but he had a magic touch when it came to evocative descriptions of the self-supporting life.

His manuscript was certainly organic; chapters would arrive in re-used envelopes tied up with string, which, when opened, brought the farmyard to the heart of the metropolis. Bits of straw and cowpat would drift down to the floor while several of the pages boasted a decorative overlay of muddy boot marks.

Not all of John's practical advice was as precise as it might have been. I decided to try out his bread-making recipe one weekend.

'Just you wait,' I said to Linda. 'When you wake up on Sunday the house will be filled with the sweet smell of freshly baked bread.'

But as I went downstairs in the morning there was no trace of the promised aroma. When I opened the oven door I found, not a seductive golden brown loaf, but a flattened rock-hard object shaped like a Frisbee which I angrily skimmed across the back garden where it thudded into a tree and startled some jackdaws.

'God, not even the birds will get any joy out of that,' I muttered.

It transpired that John's recipe had omitted a vital step in the process.

'We need to take on someone who can double-check all this stuff,' I said to Peter the next day. 'Just for three months.'

He reluctantly agreed. It was an extra cost, but we couldn't afford to have the finished books pulped because of a basic error. And judging from the response the company was getting to the first sample chapters, the print run might turn out to be significant. As we had predicted, the book was attracting interest in other European markets.

Every so often John would visit Dorling Kindersley's Covent Garden offices to go over the book's progress with the team assigned to it. Jackie Douglas, the kindly mothering figure in the group, would review the state of his clothing, pass a withering comment, and hustle him across the road to Moss Bros to replace the bits that were beyond repair. We would then go for a curry and a pint in New Row, after which John would fall asleep at one of the desks, only perking up when a particular designer who favoured short skirts and cleavage-revealing tops was innocently bent over the copying machine. We loved John dearly but he nearly drove us nuts.

The offices on the top two floors of 29 King Street were filling up. If you produce illustrated reference books characterised by deliberately complex design, which is what DK did, they inevitably require more work, and more people, than the initial estimates. Researchers, assistant editors, assistant designers, home economists were constantly being drafted in, either temporarily or permanently. The place was buzzing. And new projects were on the blocks. No sooner had *The Book of Photography* been published in the spring of 1976, and rapidly reprinted, than Peter Kindersley was demanding the development of a follow-up, a more hard-working manual. At the same time, we were beginning to plan out the first ever illustrated babycare book.

For the latter, as for much else in those early days, we were indebted to Bob Gottlieb at Knopf and Tony Schulte at Random House in New York. They were the real godfathers of DK's early years, generously bankrolling the first clutch of books on the understanding that, over time, we would refund them the portion of the costs that wouldn't be covered by the US commitment. As the foreign language contracts for a title were secured, so we progressively repaid the debt. It was an incredibly enlightened approach to helping a company get off the ground, promoted by truly decent people who were key players in a company culture that seemed admirable in every way. I used to feel that visiting the Knopf offices near the top of the Random House building on East 50th Street was one of the most pleasurable experiences it was possible to have in the publishing world. Everything about Knopf had class, understated but unmissable, from the distinguished lineage of authors to the eclectic designs of the book covers, from the variations on the borzoi colophon to the reassuring feel of the deckle-edged paper and the elegant choices of typeface. Several of the Knopf editors, especially Chuck Elliott, Kathy Hourigan, Toinette Lippe and Bobbie Bristol, who worked closely with us on shaping and improving the texts as well as adapting them for the American market, became long-term friends. They worked in a civilised, liberal atmosphere that seemed to me to represent what every publisher should aspire to and which is now, in the corporatised fever of today's conglomerates, a comparative rarity, though I don't doubt that Knopf retains its distinctive individuality.

No DK title could be contemplated unless it had, first of all, the backing of an American house. New York was, therefore, always the first port of call, and it was on one of those early trips that Bob Gottlieb suggested an author for our proposed babycare manual. Knopf had recently successfully published *Babyhood* by Penelope Leach, a semi-academic study of the first months of life, and he suggested that she might be the ideal person to develop a more practical book.

At first sight Penelope Leach did not fit the conventional preconceptions of a childcare author, being neither rounded and mumsy nor starched and bossy. A 60-a-day Hampstead intellectual with a gravelly, theatrical voice, she combined easy empathetic charm with high-voltage neurotic energy. Her writing was fluent, insightful, logical, and absolutely unstoppable. If you made a comment about the choice of a word in a sentence, she was more likely to rewrite the whole paragraph, and add in some extra material that had just sprung to mind, than simply substitute one word for another. A book that began with a target length of 352 pages emerged a year later at 512 pages – though it is true that we at DK were also complicit in this, partly because the quality of her content was so rich. The extra bulk of the book put pressure on the retail price, but fortunately this made no difference to the sales. The world of the nuclear family, where daughters had moved away from home and the traditional hearthside wisdom of mothers and grandmothers, was in need of a new bible of childcare, and here was the first illustrated example to show how to cope with the essentials of parenting. Also in its favour was that it was authored by a woman, herself a mother, and it was the first book of its kind to be written from the baby's point of view. Bob Gottlieb had been right – Knopf sold millions of *Your Baby and Child*, and Penelope Leach became the first major challenger to Benjamin Spock.

I remember the spring and summer of 1976 as being one of the most special times in all the years I spent with DK. We were still only about twenty employees, not yet big enough to cause management issues. We had survived, literally, a baptism of fire, and now the road was opening out before us. Of the first three books published, one – *The Book of Photography* – was a definite hit, while the four currently in production – *The Atlas of Early Man*, *The Complete Book of Self-Sufficiency*, *The Photographer's Handbook*, and *Baby and Child* – all felt stimulating and original, a feeling reinforced whenever Christopher and Caroline came back from sales trips to Europe where there was no shortage of customer interest. The atmosphere in the company was one of intense yet cheerful dedication, with a strong sense of camaraderie as we gathered in the early evenings of that long hot summer to sup our pints on the pavement outside the Lamb & Flag.

The Frankfurt that followed was sensational, a total contrast to the wretched conditions of the previous year. DK had a stand in Hall 5, and the reception for our books was just remarkable. Almost every market in the world vied for the rights to *Baby and Child*; every publisher who had bought *The Book of Photography* wanted *The Photographer's Handbook*; *The Atlas of Early Man* was sold in eight languages and to numerous book clubs; and there were auctions for *The Complete Book of Self-Sufficiency*. For some reason we had a problem selling the John Seymour title to the German market. I recall that I spent hours walking the German halls in search of the right publisher for it. The response was almost always the same: 'Ach, this book is absolutely so charming. Wirklich.

The foundations of DK's backlist were laid by the early investment in strong concepts and name authors such as John Seymour and Penelope Leach (pictured), John Hedgecoe and Jacquetta Hawkes.

But I'm truly sorry, I wouldn't dare to publish it. However, please, please, send me a copy – for my own personal joy, you understand.'

I did, but I didn't. If they were publishers and they liked it so much, why didn't they have the balls to acquire it? One of them even visited me in my hotel, so anxious was he to secure his personal copy, until I realised from the way his eyes were moistening under their long lashes that he had a different agenda in mind.

Eventually Walter Diem of Ravensburger agreed to take 7,500 copies, but only on condition that he could print. This was strictly against our rules of co-edition packaging – you only sold printing films rather than finished books to a publisher when there was no other way of selling that title to a market. In this instance that seemed to be the case, so we reluctantly relented. A few days after *The Complete Book of Self-Sufficiency* was published in Germany, *Der Spiegel* ran a rave double-page review. The book became a massive bestseller and John Seymour found himself an iconic figure all across the Fatherland. No doubt all those publishers who had so lamely rejected it were now unholstering their Lugers and taking a long walk in the woods.

At the end of the fair a Greek publisher, anxious to do business with us, arrived on the stand. He was wearing a heavy-duty raincoat, from whose capacious inside pockets he extracted wads of cash in various East European currencies. This was his method of paying an advance. He insisted we take the money – it was a matter of honour as well as practical business as far as he was concerned. On the drive back to

England, we stopped overnight at a modest hostelry in the Ardennes and caused much bewilderment to the proprietor by paying for our stay in an assortment of drachmas, dinars, zlotys, marks and francs.

Back in London we unloaded the VW camper van. Then the whole company crossed King Street to Penny's Place, our local wine bar (previously, and again today, the Essex Serpent pub). The celebrations lasted through the afternoon and into the early evening. When we had ordered the final bottle, the bill just nudged past the £100 mark. There's a certain nostalgia in the memory that twenty people could then get pie-eyed for a fiver a head.

Management by Hand Grenade

The company had been founded on a £10,000 overdraft, guaranteed against Peter and Christopher's homes. But this was never drawn upon. The generosity of the arrangement with Random House in the US and the remarkable strike rate of the early titles were buffers against debt. The philosophy from the start had been to create a backlist – we worked on the basis that the first round of sales would cover the origination costs of a book plus overheads, and thereafter any reprint would be clear profit. It was remarkable that we achieved a level of financial stability so quickly. By the summer of 1977, thirty months after the official launch of Dorling Kindersley, we had produced just seven books. The first two made the least impact – *The Origin of Johnny* just didn't generate sales through bookstores, and *The Taste of Wine* (subsequently, and somewhat unfairly, dubbed The Waste of Time) enjoyed only modest success. But the next five were palpable hits. *The Atlas of Early Man* would sell over 250,000 copies, while the other four – *The Book of Photography, The Complete Book of Self-Sufficiency, The Photographer's Handbook*, and *Baby and Child* – all became million-sellers, the latter two multi-million. Thus there was a constant stream of reprint income being generated all round the world, all of which was ploughed into funding the next raft of titles rather than into any fancy upgrading of the offices or personal frippery for the principals.

When it came to the principals, two more diverse characters would be hard to imagine. Christopher Dorling was easy-going, laid-back, soft spoken, slightly eccentric and generally content to sit and observe the scene unfolding around him before removing his pipe and offering what was often a telling and slightly unexpected opinion. I used to think that perhaps this was one of the benefits of a Quaker upbringing. He had engaging foibles, too, such as a firm belief in the virtues of sliced white bread at a time when the chattering classes were rising in rebellion against it and demanding rustic artisanal wholemeal. Caroline Oakes (then his partner, later his wife) was already a fervent advocate of health foods and alternative therapies and it was amusing to hear her try to break down his defence of the orthodox. Christopher's chief focus in those days was on the management of production and, with Caroline, of co-edition sales. His knowledge of the latter, mostly acquired from travelling with James Mitchell, was invaluable, and DK would never have been able to start without it.

While Christopher was calm and reflective, Peter Kindersley was volatility personified. He was really two people. On the one hand, as the son of David Kindersley, the celebrated letter-cutter and sculptor, he had been partially home-schooled in the free-range, smock-and-sandals environment of the Eric Gill fraternity. From this he had matured into a perfectionist craftsman, and this side of him manifested itself in a generous, companionable way that was genuinely endearing. The other Peter was the ruthless, driven, commercially minded achiever who would allow nothing to deflect him from attaining his goals. The problem for everyone working with him was that you never knew which Peter was going to turn up. There were days when he would arrive at the office with tight lips and a jaundiced cast to his eyes. On such mornings it was wise to keep a distance until the hurricane had blown over. All over the building it was possible to hear the explosions from his desk as some hapless individual was eviscerated for some minor transgression. But once the tempest had cleared, he could switch in an instant to a forgiving sweetness.

'Unbelievable!' said one wannabe author as I consoled him over a beer after he had been vapourised. 'I never met anyone before who could be so charming and such a shit in the same sentence.'

'Yes,' I said. 'We call it "management by hand grenade". It keeps you on your toes, that's for sure.'

But both sides of Peter's personality benefited the company. From Peter the Craftsman came the mantra inherited from his father: 'If a job is worth doing, it is worth doing well.' Thus nothing could ever be produced by the company that did not meet with Peter's aesthetic satisfaction, not even a party invitation or a Christmas card. The design, the typography, the images – all had to be in immaculate conjunction. And woe betide the designer who presented him with a sans-serif typeface. He would react as if a dog had thrown up at his feet.

Peter the Ruthless engendered the spirit of always looking forward, never looking back. While the rest of us were tempted to bask in the success of the early titles, he was cracking the whip to come up with more and better ideas. Complacency was verboten. He was unsparing in his treatment of anyone whom he considered a passenger, following the principle of migrating birds that peck to death the stragglers impeding their progress. The single-mindedness came from complete self-confidence, in his vision and in its execution. It was scary, sometimes infuriating, but ultimately inspiring.

Working for, and with, Peter was a challenge. If you didn't develop the hide of an elephant in the face of his blistering critiques, you wouldn't make it. There were, for example, two of the most talented book designers in the country in the positions of art directors at DK – Roger Bristow and Stuart Jackman. For some reason they suffered the most from Peter's abuse, yet they were among the people he most admired for their talents. Every year, on our journeys by car to Frankfurt, Stuart, no doubt exhausted from the pre-book fair madness, would fall into a depressed state and threaten to give up after Peter had picked holes in the stand design or the dummy sales materials. But he usually bounced back once we had collectively reassured him of his value to the company. Roger, on the other hand, became over the years so browbeaten by the hail of criticism that he eventually threw in the towel and left the company, which was a real loss to the creative strength of DK.

The keys to surviving the working week with Peter were a) not to take criticism personally, and b) to stand up for yourself. He would usually back off from direct confrontation. It is nevertheless a tribute to his inspirational qualities that so many employees stayed loyal to the company for years. They took the pragmatic view that here was a leader who was taking the business forward, and to follow in his footsteps would outweigh any personal pain inflicted by his barbs. There was also the undeniable truth that in the decisions he took he was right at least 90 per cent of the time. Long before it became the tag line for Nike, Peter's standard command of 'Just Do It!' signalled the end of any resistance to what one considered a questionable course of action. Later, he was usually proved to have been astute in his judgment.

Christopher Dorling and Peter Kindersley
in the back room office at 9 Henrietta Street.

There was, however, one notable weakness in his armoury, and that was an inability to handle dissent if it came from a group rather than an individual. In those early days everyone was working fiendishly long hours. By the time a book was completed and ready for press, the creative team was clearly burned out. Home relationships were suffering, and it was almost impossible to find the moment to squeeze in a holiday. Inevitably the question of overtime came up, along with other rights being implemented by publishing houses at the time, including maternity and paternity leave. The NUJ was still a force in the business and some DK staff were members.

Peter had a bizarre, old-fashioned paranoia about the NUJ. He refused to meet with a small group of staff who wanted to discuss whether various benefits could be built into their contracts. He said, in as many words, that if a union was set up, he would close the company down and start again. And I'm sure he meant it. Christopher sat back and smoked his pipe. It fell to me to act as an intermediary between staff and management, a task I didn't especially relish.

In the end it worked out reasonably well. The staff, even the most vociferous rebels, believed in DK and wanted to play a part in its future. I managed to head off the threat of a union being formed by consulting *The Journal*, the organ of the NUJ, which listed all the benefits negotiated with various houses. I made a judgment as to what was reasonable as well as affordable, consulted with Peter and Christopher, and offered the package to the staff. In place of a union they could form a staff committee. The compromise seemed to work. We even started a crèche in Covent Garden. From that moment, in addition to my role as editorial director, I became an unofficial personnel director, a situation that lasted until we hired a proper HR director some 15 years later, by which time the company had grown to a size way beyond my modest capabilities of people management and way beyond the time we needed such a department.

There was one key benefit we introduced early on that was widely appreciated and became a vital element in the company culture. This was a profit-sharing scheme that involved everyone – as long as the profits were there to be shared. While it was based on seniority and length of service, the priority was to reward those on the bottom rungs of the pay scale first. It was tough enough then, as it still is today, to live in London on a basic publishing salary, so even in years when profits weren't sufficiently large to be able to reward everyone, the staff below management level always received a handout. Even when we became a public company, there were years when the holding board directors took no bonus but the staff did. It was a shock to me to find years later, after DK had been taken over by Pearson, that their bonus system worked in precisely the opposite way and Penguin board meetings devoted much time to the percentages senior people could anticipate in a given year. I believe that one of the reasons DK engendered such fierce staff loyalty was that the company cared in this way about its people. If you are not sitting on the backlist of some giant of literature, the employees working for a publishing, or packaging, company are really its only asset. This seemed self-evident to me all through my publishing life, and even more so when we became a plc where so much emphasis is noisily put on satisfying shareholders. I believe, as Richard Branson does, that if you look after your staff, they will look after the product, the product will then satisfy the customers, and the sales will benefit the shareholders.

To be accurate, the people weren't the only asset at DK. From the outset, the company philosophy had been, as far as possible, to own what we produced. The aim was to build a library of content that could be exploited in future publications and, many years later, on other platforms. Artworks were commissioned for titles, and then stored in trunks. Later, when the use of photography became extensive in DK books, this was accumulated in a picture library. And author contracts specified that their text could be used in multiple formats, while allowing them to retain copyright.

It was a far-sighted approach but a necessary one as the costs of originating the complex page designs so favoured by Peter Kindersley were invariably high. And they always went higher than budget, partly because of the extra staff needed to bring in a book on schedule, partly because writers or illustrators or photographers were invariably late, and partly because of the "PK fiddle factor" which could entail breathtaking about-turns at crucial points in the title's production. On one occasion, a book about to be dispatched to the printer was held back because he decided that he would prefer it to be set in a different typeface. His aesthetic judgment may have been right, but the budget went north.

The issue of producing books within budget became one of the most frequently revisited issues over the years and I don't believe it was ever satisfactorily resolved. There were always the opposing forces of prudence and perfection. And there were conflicting views coming from the top. On one occasion, a young editor, new to the company, was covering galleys with blue pencil in order to make the text fit on the page. Peter Kindersley appeared at his shoulder and winced. The editor, in trepidation, asked him if he was worried by the extra costs being incurred by corrections.

'Don't worry' said Peter, 'I have a formula for typesetting. You get a quotation and then double it.'

On the other hand, when Peter was asked on a different occasion how the editors should approach budgets, his advice was 'to think of the money we were spending as if it was our own – and then remember that it isn't.' Ultimately, whenever it came down to a tussle on the page between the cost and the pursuit of excellence, the latter was always the winner.

Nobody could deny that such attention to quality was admirable. It was always the first word that came to mind when people spoke about DK. Quality was uppermost in the core values that were drilled into us day after day. Another was to ensure the book was accessible, in the most user-friendly way, to the reader. If a topic or a process could be more easily grasped by the use of illustration, then supply it and don't leave the reader floundering in a dense paragraph of text, as was the custom with traditional publishers unwilling or unable to afford photographs or drawings.

It was a given that a book had to be market-led. What did people need to know? Were they being well served by existing books on the subject? How could we create one that would serve them better – and, at the same time, offer them real value for money? This was the process that initiated the thinking about a new topic. Then the other values could be overlaid. In addition to the virtues of quality and accessibility, the book would need to have some unique selling point to differentiate it from the competition. This was the core challenge at the outset and the reason for so much time being spent on developing sample pages to present to the international markets. The unique selling point had to be there, highly visible to the potential buyer, compelling, seductive, and justifiable.

The next value to be applied was authority. The reader would need to be sure that the information inside was reliable. Usually this trust was conferred either by a known author in the field or by an institution whose imprimatur would be recognised as the ultimate endorsement. A further consideration was the necessity of creating the content in a way that could work for any market in the world. Pictures with backgrounds that portrayed a national or class bias were to be avoided – the information had to be presented in a neutral way so that a reader in Stockholm or Sydney or Sarajevo would not think it an alien import. This was a discipline every editor and designer had to learn until it became second nature to them.

But perhaps the most striking – to me – of all the DK values was Peter's insistence that the books combine the elements of beauty and usefulness. This clearly came from his father's Arts and Crafts influence. It was a simple yet compelling concept. Imagine a water jug. If it is well designed so that the water pours easily in a smooth stream, then it is useful. But, when adorning a shelf, it can also be an object of beauty. Why should an everyday object be ugly? His aim therefore with every DK title we produced was to create a book that people would want to pick up and admire because of its attractive qualities, and then find that the information within was precisely what they needed to know to improve some aspect of their lives. This conjunction of the aesthetic and the practical was the principal reason we hated having the term "coffee table" applied to the list. To us, coffee table books were usually just decorative furnishings.

9 Henrietta Street

The ultimate good luck of being in the right place at the right time was certainly mine at the outset of Dorling Kindersley. In those days, when we were small, and before we had a full-scale international sales team, those of us engaged in the origination of the books were also involved in the selling of them. There is no better education to be had in understanding the different markets around the world than from travelling to them with ideas to show. You can't always trust a publisher's word but such is the sense of self-importance which attaches itself to the position, you can be damn sure they will always give you the benefit of their opinion. Whether or not you agreed with them, it was always worth listening, and during a two- or three-day trip round a medley of houses in any given country or city, you were certain to return to base with informed views about which of the projects were right for the market, how they might be improved, and, for the future, other topics which could benefit from a DK treatment. Over time I became convinced that the selling of the books was in fact the making of them, and as the company grew bigger and employed international sales people, it was a source of regret that not all of the editors who joined could have the opportunity to profit from such a learning curve.

Peter and Christopher recognised, too, the importance of nurturing strong alliances around the world. In the US the key relationship was with the Random House group, to such a degree that by the time we launched as a publisher over there in 1991, 50 per cent of our US backlist was with one or other of its imprints. The second most important market in the mid-'70s was, briefly, Holland – the demand for illustrated books there was greater even than in France or Germany. All the Dutch publishers competed to have one of their titles selected as a Book of the Month, a national promotion that ensured every bookstore across the country took a bulk quantity and displayed it prominently at an attractive discount. They used to shift 90,000 copies in a few weeks. Holland was known as "the guilder pipeline" while the good times rolled. In the UK Ebury Press, as the publisher of our photography list, became a significant partner, as did Larousse in France for the same reason. In Sweden we developed a strong relationship with the Bonnier group, under Bo Streiffert; in Norway Aschehoug, on the back of early successes with DK titles, sought (unsuccessfully) to have an exclusive agreement with us; and in Italy Enzo Angelucci at Mondadori acted as a patriarchal godfather to us. This developed into a dual relationship as Mondadori would soon feature large in our lives as both publisher and printer. As for Japan, Tom Mori was setting up his Tuttle-Mori agency at the same time as DK was starting out; he too stayed in some starless hotel in Frankfurt's seamy quarter in the early days. He became a wonderful friend to us and, with Yuji Takeda, ensured we secured a foothold in that market.

The key, however, to maximising sales in a market was to tap into the channels outside the book trade. But you couldn't necessarily rely on a publisher who was buying in a book that hadn't been produced internally and therefore had no editor to own it in the way he or she would own one of their home-grown titles, to devote energy to exploring additional sales possibilities. The well known "not invented here" principle applied. We had to do the legwork ourselves. In the 1970s and '80s the reach and range of the book clubs was phenomenal. In the UK and Holland, for example, you could expect print runs of 100,000 copies for a main selection; France might deliver more; while Germany, the most powerful book club market of all, could command quantities of 200,000-300,000 copies. Even at their heavily discounted buy-in prices, to secure one of these slots was a substantial prize and could additionally make a significant difference to the printing margins – as long as you retained the right to manufacture, a never-ending battle but one we seldom lost. We were tenacious in pursuing such deals and diligent in building relationships with the key players in the clubs, to such an extent that on at least four occasions we were commissioned by Bertelsmann's French, German and Austrian clubs to create main selections for them from scratch. With the right to license these titles to the rest of the world, these were sweet deals indeed.

Even more potent than the book clubs then were the giant direct mail marketing machines of Reader's Digest and Time-Life. The former loomed large in our lives because it had begun producing big handsomely designed household reference books in the UK at about the same time as Mitchell Beazley was set up, which gave rise to a somewhat acidic rivalry that later extended to DK. Reader's Digest only produced about six major titles a year, but because they had been market-tested to the nth degree, a major print run was guaranteed and they could afford to spend the time and the money on getting each book exactly right for their readership, which could broadly be summed up as the middle-aged middle classes of middle England. The year-on-year success of the UK office induced among its management a patrician disdain for the more rapidly assembled works of its rivals, and there seemed little chance of DK ever being in the frame for a cooperative venture.

Fortunately for us, a benign couple in RD's US office, John Pope and Stewart Downing, took notice of our stand at Frankfurt, admired the quality of our books, and because they didn't have the in-house capacity to create it for themselves, commissioned DK to produce for them a comprehensive guide to houseplants. This was a major breakthrough. It brought an entirely new discipline to the house – we had to learn to work to RD specifications and standards, in particular their house style of editing which involved the text being submitted, like very muddy clothing, to a series of washes until it had been cleansed of every tiny wrinkle of opinion or ambiguity. The end result was a prose style homogenised to such a degree that it had not a shred of personality and was in effect as lifeless as a bag of laundry. But it was clear that this conservative fail-safe approach to household reference served their market admirably. Above all, it avoided the risk of having to pulp an enormous print run because a reader had been misled by a carelessly worded instruction. A basic error could wipe away your profits in an instant, as one major New York house discovered when it launched a cookbook with a massive first printing. Unfortunately the instruction to boil a can of beans in a pan omitted the direction to 'add water to the pan'. Some hapless reader wrote in to complain that she had been sideswiped by a can of beans exploding all over her kitchen, and a quarter of a million books were recalled by the publisher to be pulped.

We were lucky in that we had from the early days retained the freelance services of a veteran American editor of the old school. Donald Berwick had little innate flair as a writer, but as an editor he was absolutely first rate at reworking a text until it was fit for purpose. He became a wonderful mentor to all of us, and he stayed to work on many of our large-scale reference works until age and deafness defeated him. He became the bridge between DK and the Digest on *Success with Houseplants*, and his presence gave RD the confidence to continue working with us.

Success with Houseplants was the first in a series of major DK reference books to appear under the banner of household brands over the next three years. In parallel with the RD title, a sizeable team was creating *The Good Housekeeping Encyclopedia of Needlecraft*, a stitch-by-stitch illustrated guide to every aspect of the subject, while in another part of the building

The Good Housekeeping Step-by-Step Cookbook was being assembled, and a fourth team was beginning work on what would become, in the US, *The American Medical Association Family Medical Guide*. Between them, these books accounted for some 2,000 pages of intensely worked practical guidance that had to be checked and double-checked by the sponsoring authority. They were time-consuming to make and very costly because of the number of people required to work on them. The company's staff more than doubled.

By 1978 we had outgrown the few floors we occupied at the top of 29 King Street and needed to find larger premises. There were a couple of decent middle-range restaurants left in the market area when it was relocated: The Grange in King Street and its sister, The Garden, at No 9 Henrietta Street. Now, the latter had closed and the building was available to let, with the proviso that the ground floor continue to be a retail outlet. So David Kindersley, Peter's father, created a handsome nameplate for the front in joined-up gold lettering which proclaimed Dorling Kindersley Limited, Publishers and Booksellers. We weren't actually either – all our books then were packaged and appeared in the UK under the imprints of traditional publishers. And, anyway, by the time we moved into Henrietta Street, we had produced only fifteen titles, so it was a stretch to call ourselves Booksellers. But that is how we circumvented the retail restriction – the reception area at the front of the building was ringed with bookcases on which our miscellany of fifteen titles was displayed for sale. My memory is hazy as to whether we ever sold any of those books. If we did, the proceeds undoubtedly went into a petty cash box in the receptionist's desk and probably paid for some lunchtime sandwiches.

The back office, on the ground floor, was a pleasant room with a skylight that gave it an airy feel in the daytime. It had previously contained the bar for pre-dinner cocktails. Now it housed the four directors of DK – Peter, Christopher, Caroline, myself – in a space intimate enough for the exchange of information when the atmosphere was collegiate but too close for comfort when it was chilly. As usual, the collective mood of the room emanated from where Peter sat. Christopher managed to insulate himself behind a tall bookcase placed between him and Peter. Caroline, who unfortunately suffered from the latter's under-appreciation of her efforts (he probably assumed, mistakenly, that she was only in the role of international sales director because she was Christopher's partner) sat diagonally across from him. To avoid being zapped by his rays she strategically placed a large broad-leaved houseplant to cut across his line of vision. As for myself, I was face-to-face with him without a fig leaf of protection or privacy.

In the middle of the room was an antique, round, slightly wobbly table, which became the emblem for the company's creative gestation. The door to the office was always open – to everyone. Designers and editors would bring work in progress to be laid out on the round table and discussed; production staff would give feedback on manufacturing negotiations; international sales people would report on trips; and authors, illustrators, photographers, agents, and visiting publishers would sit at the table to pitch or be pitched at. In this way, all four of us kept abreast of what was happening in the company, even if we weren't directly involved in the meeting at the centre of the room.

The stairway down to the basement, where the main dining area had been, was a David Hicks creation, the only surviving feature of his work on the restaurant design. At one end of this dark windowless space a bricked-in area was designated as the boardroom, though it quickly became known as The Bunker, not just because Peter was frequently referred to as the Führer, but also because he was for ever urging illustrators to recreate Hitler's actual bunker for him. It was one of the few commands that were successfully resisted for more than a quarter of a century.

At the other end of the basement was the kitchen, now appropriated by the team responsible for the *Good Housekeeping Step-by-Step Cookbook* for which the US and UK editions had to be created in parallel. Every recipe had to be cooked and tested, first in UK measurements and ingredients, then in the US equivalents, and then photographed. With over 1,000 recipes and 6,000 illustrations, this was a mammoth undertaking. Every day the smells of cooking permeated up through the building, tempting hungry opportunists down at lunchtime to see if there were free pickings to be snaffled, though you had to be careful what you chose. You didn't necessarily want to sample the meatloaf if the photographer had applied an aerosol spray to give it that perfect sheen as it nestled in the gravy…

The five floors of the handsome 18th-century building were now teeming with DK's workforce. Upstairs the elegant panelled rooms, before whose fireplaces men in boots and breeches had once toasted their superior backsides, were filled with the random detritus of a publishing house as editors, designers, production managers, accountants and foreign rights personnel scurried to occupy every available working space.

In the room where *The Good Housekeeping Encyclopedia of Needlecraft* was being produced, bright young graduates with impressive degrees in the humanities were to be found sitting at desks surrounded by skeins of wool, holding knitting needles and a single row of stitched sweater while a photographer captured every individual step of the process. In another room, where *The AMA Family Medical Guide* was in progress, a more sickly-looking group was evidently suffering from too much exposure to the variety of ailments for which a symptom might be a clue. And, in a third crowded space, some harassed editors were rewriting for the seventeenth time the caption to watering a ficus or propagating a pilea.

I occasionally felt guilty that these starry-eyed graduates whom we had recently recruited were spending the first year of their publishing lives on such mentally unchallenging tasks. Before *The Times* newspaper modernised itself, the place to look for job openings was on its quirky back page. A small ad placed there with the enticing heading "Fancy a Career in Publishing?" had generated 600 replies. Culling the majority wasn't difficult – those that couldn't write, couldn't spell, couldn't express themselves succinctly or compellingly, or just sounded plain wrong, were binned. A second round eliminated the predictably dull and the obviously dilettante.

We probably interviewed about 30 and eventually selected five. (Among those five were Fiona MacIntyre, now MD at Ebury, and David Lamb, now Publisher at Mitchell Beazley.) After winning medals in the marathon selection process, the successful candidates found themselves in a Covent Garden sweatshop trying to fit the caption to "How to bake a tarte tatin" into three short lines.

The recent graduates from the art schools, which we also raided for promising graphic designers, were similarly head down in the painstaking minutiae of step-by-step illustrated sequences. But they, like the novitiate editors, seemed quite unfazed. The simple truth was that DK was a stimulating place to work. It was young-minded, aspirational, unhierarchical and obviously going places. Just to come through the front door and into the reception area was to inhale an atmosphere of restless promise. And if you found yourself in a job there, the chances were high that you would stick around for a while.

Sex in the Connaught

If ever the staff wondered if it was worth their while to be embedded in such major projects for such a length of time, their diligence was rewarded soon after publication. Just as four of our first seven titles had given us a platform to grow, now this new clutch of home reference found its niche. By the early 1980s we had chalked up four more global bestsellers that would calcify into pillars of the backlist: *The Good Housekeeping Encyclopedia of Needlecraft* sold over 500,000 copies, *The Good Housekeeping Step-by-Step Cookbook* more than a million, *Success with Houseplants* more than two million, and *The AMA Family Medical Guide*, thanks to it being selected by Reader's Digest USA for a mailing, sold twice as many again. It was no less than the teams deserved for their dedication to creating the best possible books on the subject in a very crowded market, just as international success was a testament to the legwork put in by the sales people around the world. At the centre was Peter and Christopher's drive to secure and maintain a core relationship with the presiding imprimaturs of the titles – Reader's Digest, Good Housekeeping, and the American Medical Association.

In many ways, dealing with the latter was the hardest task of all as it involved a complicated four-way relationship between Dorling Kindersley (based in London), Random House, the US publisher (based in New York), John Cushman, the AMA's agent (also based in New York), and the AMA themselves (based in Chicago). The AMA's name was not held in high public esteem when the book was published in the US in 1982. As a traditionally minded conservative rampart of the medical establishment its senior figures were inclined to fall back into defensive postures in the face of public criticism. They weren't exactly falling over themselves in delight when they discovered that a core manual bearing their illustrious name would be produced by a bunch of unknowns who weren't even American. There were also the damaged egos of their own in-house books department to massage, something that I doubt was ever achieved to their satisfaction. John Cushman and Tony Wimpfheimer (the senior Random House publisher in charge of the book) did their best to charm their way through but Kindersley was no masseur. He just saw those who raised objections as donkeys blocking his path. It was never less than a battleground between him and the AMA books team, not even when the finished article proved to be a groundbreaking success and at the same time restored respectability to their imprimatur.

The AMA Family Medical Guide was a prime example of a household reference work where we found a Unique Selling

Point at the outset to give it an edge over the competition. This took the form of diagnostic charts, or algorithms, from which the reader could determine whether a common symptom needed medical attention or not. The idea came to us by chance from somebody who had witnessed barefoot doctors (as they were called) in East Africa being trained to use simple diagnostic charts on their visits to distant villages in the bush. From these charts they could make a judgment as to whether, for example, a person with a stomach ache was more likely to be suffering from a) indigestion, b) appendicitis or c) something more serious. The creation of such charts in a more sophisticated form for the book, and with multiple cross-references to supporting articles, was highly complex, but it proved a winning formula. It was the feature that persuaded the AMA to come on board.

Despite the somewhat corrosive atmosphere between DK and the AMA books team, we subsequently collaborated on an *A-Z Encyclopedia of Medicine*, which also proved a formidable seller, and for this in the UK we acquired the British Medical Association as a partner, a relationship that was by contrast a model of cooperative harmony. For that we owe a great debt of thanks to Dr Tony Smith who spent many years working alongside the editors, advising and guiding them through these massive books and their subsequent revised editions with patience, good humour and a light ironic touch. He was a key player in creating the bridge that linked DK with the BMA.

Thus the backlist became the powerhouse at the core of the company's creative expansion, fuelling investment in new projects at least until these were covered by advances from acquiring publishers, and safeguarding us from the fallout of books that failed. There were a few of the latter – a batch of middle-range titles published around the same time as the big reference books performed only modestly. Their origination costs might have been covered but they were not reprinting and were therefore, in our terms, not contributing to growth or profits. We needed the buffer of the big gorillas.

We also needed to shore up our list with more frontline authors, especially since we had suffered one major defection. Having, with the help of Adrian Bailey as his amanuensis on *The Book of Photography* and Michael Langford in a similar role on *The Photographer's Handbook*, authored the two most successful books on the subject ever published, John Hedgecoe was courted by James Mitchell, who had apparently overcome his own myopia about the photography market. Hedgecoe was seduced into the arms of Mitchell Beazley, no doubt for many fistfuls of moolah. There is no more self-inflated sound than that of a Porsche engine being revved in a London street, as Adrian Bailey described his encounter one day with a gleaming new machine from which stepped the irrepressible Hog (as he was known in house).

'You want to get yourself another publisher, Adrian,' was John's taunting line before roaring away in a cloud of smoke.

(In fact, Adrian privately agreed with Hedgecoe, but for very different reasons. The mildest of men, he later startled me by admitting that if he ever bumped into Peter Kindersley again, he might have to be physically restrained from throttling him.)

While it was annoying to lose John, we had the best of his books which Mitchell Beazley could never match, and on the back of those we built a photographic list of nineteen titles which served us admirably until the SLR boom fizzled out. Years later, when MB's fortunes had declined, John came back, and together we revived his original book. And despite his spluttering contempt for its artlessness, he even produced a title on digital photography.

In any event Hedgecoe's departure was more than mitigated by the arrival of three other authors who would prove invaluable acquisitions both for the frontlist and the backlist. Penelope Leach had successfully breached a hole in the male-dominated wall of babycare publishing, so we searched for the expertise of a woman, and a mother, who could do the same for pregnancy and childbirth. Sheila Kitzinger had acquired an instant reputation with her first book, *The Experience of Childbirth*, published in the late '50s, and she was well known in the UK as a founder of the National Childbirth Trust, and internationally for her lectures on the rights of women to choose their preferred birth methods. She agreed to author *Pregnancy and Childbirth* for us, a comprehensive handbook which we issued in the same format as the Leach manual, and once again we found publishers around the world eager to adopt the title. Knopf, in the US, had another big seller from DK.

It was fun working with Sheila. She was frank, uninhibited, wise, compassionate and unshockable, and visiting her at her manor house near Oxford was like paying court to the great Earth Mother Goddess herself. We collaborated on a number of titles over the years, including a wonderful book for children called *Being Born* in which we married her poetic text with the remarkable intra-uterine photography of Lennart Nilsson (a co-venture with Bo Streiffert, formerly Nilsson's publisher at Bonnier). Before that, however, she had made waves with *A Woman's Experience of Sex*, which she, as the mother of four daughters, had initiated and on which some of them provided useful input. It was pretty bold for its time and generated a major auction for the rights among US publishers – though, sadly, the actual sales there fell short of expectations.

When Sheila first proposed the idea, she suggested we meet early in the day somewhere between Paddington Station and Covent Garden. We settled on the Connaught, which was then a byword for stuffiness but renowned for its breakfast. Jackie Douglas, into whose area the book would fall, was with me. As we gently probed Sheila for her ideas about how the book would develop and what form the illustrations could take, her voice rose higher and higher as she became more animated about what she wanted to express. At some point she began describing the experience of multiple orgasms at a decibel level which, like Meg Ryan in the restaurant scene, caused a hush to settle in the gloom of the Connaught dining room. All at once several copies of *The Times* were lowered and our table became the focal point of disbelieving glares. A classic Bateman cartoon. Then, after a noisy shake, the newspapers were raised again and the starched shirts behind them continued to masticate on toast and Oxford marmalade. But Sheila wasn't giving in to any social niceties. She went on, equally loudly, to pronounce on masturbation, the differences between clitoral and vaginal orgasms, and the art of giving oral sex. By the time we had got onto the role played by turkey basters in lesbian pregnancies, the dining room had conspicuously emptied. A pity. The old sticks who walked out might have learned something. They looked like inveterate missionary positioners.

Thereafter the universal perennials of sex, pregnancy and childcare became rich seams of the company's publishing programme, to which Miriam Stoppard brought a glamorous lustre when she became a DK author. Miriam was a vital signing for us – her output over more than a quarter of a century has been prolific, many of her titles have been bestsellers, and her constantly renewable backlist has provided a core bedrock of revenue year on year. Of all the authors contracted by DK in its history, Miriam has been by some distance the most loyal and the most productive. The credit for coaxing her to DK in the first place belongs to Amy Carroll, an unquiet American who joined us as a part-time typist when we were in Kennington and swiftly rose to be an entrepreneurial managing editor with a clear eye for a commercial opportunity. For her first book for DK Amy commissioned Miriam to write *Everywoman's Lifeguide*, a reassuringly positive manual perfectly pitched for the zeitgeist of the early '80s.

Everywoman's Lifeguide was one of the last books DK produced as a packager in the UK market. It was sold to Anthony Cheetham and Carol O'Brien at Macdonald, but it was nearly strangled at birth. By the time the book was printed and ready to ship to the UK from Italy, Robert Maxwell had taken charge of Macdonald and Anthony Cheetham had moved on. Soon after, the telephone rang on Christopher Dorling's desk. I saw him pick up the receiver and then hold it out at some distance from his ear. Across the room I could hear the rumble of that intimidating basso profundo. The Bouncing Czech was trying to bounce our book back to us, claiming it was a contract that should never have been signed, etc, etc. On and on he droned like a Lancaster bomber as he tried to cower Christopher into submission with his blustery threats. Christopher was unmoved. He removed his pipe, placed it on the ashtray, and calmly pointed out that 15,000 copies of the book with the Macdonald imprint on them were now on the high seas, that he was under no circumstances going to ask for them to be returned to port, and that we expected prompt payment on delivery according to the terms of our legally binding agreement. Then he put the phone down. We never heard from the monster again.

Even if Robert Maxwell had bullied DK into reversing that contract, he would still have had to deal with Miriam Stoppard. And he would have lost. Behind her sweet exterior lies a will of unbending steel. When negotiating she combines great charm with piercing directness; she knows what she wants and she has marshalled all the arguments necessary to achieve her goal. It is hard to best her, as Peter Kindersley later discovered when she and Felicity Bryan, her agent, were arguing for a higher percentage on DK's US sales on the grounds that Miriam had become an extremely valuable asset to the company. There was no question that we could not afford to lose her to a competitor, so we were negotiating a multi-book contract that would extend over several years.

However, on the US royalty split Peter was adamant that we would make no further concession. The discussion reached a stalemate. Miriam was mystified by Peter's stance.

'Peter,' she asked, 'have you ever had to undertake a course in negotiating?'

'No. Why?'

'Well, I have. We all had to do a course at Syntex.' This was the US pharmaceutical company of which Miriam was currently CEO. 'And I'm going to show you how it is done.'

She and Felicity then left the room to consult. Peter, Amy Carroll and myself were left to reconsider our options. When the meeting reconvened, Miriam's irrefutable logic completely outflanked us. Peter had to concede defeat.

'So,' said Miriam, rising gracefully from the table in all her technicolour finery and gazing triumphantly down on her monochrome publishers in their sneakers and jeans, 'I assume you've got some champagne on ice?'

On another occasion she completely floored Peter with her uninhibited frankness. We were discussing the content of *The Breast Book*, which Miriam was about to write.

'Miriam,' said Peter, 'we really want this book to concentrate on health issues, medical treatments and so forth, and not on the sexual side of breasts.'

'But, Peter,' exclaimed Miriam in ringing tones that could be heard several rooms away, 'don't you know that millions of women worldwide experience orgasms from nipple manipulation alone?'

He had no answer to that. Once again she had got her way.

The third stellar author to join us in the early 1980s was Gerald Durrell. It was a very astute move by Joss Pearson, also a managing editor, to propose to Gerry that DK could produce for him, and with him, the kind of illustrated practical guide to natural history that his own publishers, Collins, wouldn't have the will or the resources to create. The idea was to explore the world by habitat and leaven the core information with an infusion of the anecdotal charm for which the author was universally loved.

The Amateur Naturalist was a beautiful book, and it successfully married the key Durrell ingredients of humour and acute observation with the straightforward reference material supplied by Gerry's wife, Lee. But there was another factor which helped to make it a winner in the coedition markets – DK's new style of overhead photography.

In 1980 DK had produced a breakthrough title – *The Book of Ingredients*. It didn't set the world alight with its sales, which were relatively modest, but it's a fair bet that almost every art director in the land acquired a copy. The innovation was to create a catalogue of cooking ingredients with every object – fruit, vegetables, meat, fish, spices, herbs, etc – photographed from above and displayed (life size wherever possible) on a white background. It was the first time we had used photography as opposed to artwork as a graphic form of representation. The pages may look dated now but they were highly arresting at the time.

The art director on that project was Stuart Jackman and the photographer was Philip Dowell. Now the two of them combined again to create the most illuminating double-page spreads in *The Amateur Naturalist*, the garnered pickings from a day's foraging with Gerry Durrell in a particular habitat which were carefully arranged on a white sheet and photographed from above while they retained their freshly picked lustre. It was an education in itself to accompany Gerry on these walks – along a hedgerow, a seashore, a stretch of moorland, beside a fast-running stream, or in the tinder-dry garrigue surrounding his home in the South of France. A walking nature detective, he would see things that our untrained eyes could never spot, tiny clues to the everyday cycles of life, which he would delicately gather up for inclusion in the collection to be photographed. These might be fragments of bone, owl pellets, a nipped-off bird's feather, the burrow of a beetle, the pupa of a moth, the holes drilled by shipworms in a piece of driftwood. These objets trouvés may not sound immediately photogenic but, when assembled together with the other findings from the habitat and laid out on a page with captions alongside each one, they were transformed into a captivating ensemble that intrigued and enchanted young and old alike.

Gerry Durrell was an amusing and inspiring figure, especially when encountered at his remarkable zoo on Jersey. But it wasn't always easy to synchronise with his moods, which tended to fluctuate through the day. His body clock worked in a different time zone to the rest of us, as we discovered when we first visited him in his mas outside Nîmes. We arrived after breakfast and when asked what we would like to drink, requested coffee. Gerry, however, as was his wont, had been up since five o'clock when he practised his yoga, and was now opening his first beer of the day. By mid-morning, when we

Gerald Durrell, Sheila Kitzinger and Miriam Stoppard have all authored global bestsellers for DK – in Miriam's case many times over, as she has been the company's leading author for almost 30 years.

were on our second round of coffee, he had moved on to wine, and by lunchtime to brandy. In the hot sun, sitting round a table under the vine-covered trellis in his garden, it was difficult to resist his hospitality – he was also an excellent cook – and to remember that we were going to be there for a limited time in which to establish how the book should proceed and the practicalities of getting it all done. It quickly became apparent that we would have to arrive early each morning and pack in as much work as we could before lunch. Gerry liked people to drink with him. Those of the group who could, more or less, keep pace with him found favour in his eyes, which was useful for the working relationship but punishing on the liver; those who didn't drink risked being scorned or ignored. Thus the chances of there being good chemistry between Gerry and Peter Kindersley were minimal.

Subsequently, there was chemistry between them. It was volcanic. Peter was determined that the concept of *The Amateur Naturalist* would not be confined to the pages of a book. He believed it had the potential to be a major television series and furthermore that DK, being the copyright holders to the compilation of the work, would produce it. It didn't faze him for a minute that we had no experience of the medium and no credentials to support our pitch – he would find people who did. DK Television was formed, and Jonathan Harris, an engagingly phlegmatic character with a dry sense of humour, was hired from the BBC to run this fledgling operation.

This did not sit well with Gerry Durrell nor with Dick Odgers, who was responsible for film and TV rights at Curtis Brown. They had their own ideas about how the television adaptation should be made and were appalled at the prospect of having to include Peter Kindersley in the negotiations. Ultimately a compromise was reached – DK became a co-producer, and Jonathan Harris, with whom Gerry struck up a fast friendship, directed the thirteen-part series, which was screened by Channel 4. But Channel 4 was then in its infancy and its audience levels were modest, so any hopes we nurtured about *The Amateur Naturalist* following in the footsteps of David Attenborough's *Life on Earth* with huge sales of the tie-in book were alas misplaced.

The book had been the subject of an auction in the UK, which, rather to the dismay of Gerald Durrell, was not won by Collins, his long-term publisher, but by Penelope Hoare at Hamish Hamilton. In hindsight we wondered whether Collins, with their formidable sales force and their track record with Gerry, wouldn't have made it into the bestseller it never quite became. Certainly they would have known how best to market and sell it, which wasn't immediately apparent to us from our brief encounter with Christopher Sinclair-Stevenson, then the CEO of Hamish Hamilton.

Elsewhere in the world, notably in the US (Knopf again) and in Germany, where it sold over 250,000 copies, the book was very successful. The German edition was bolstered by a foreword from Konrad Lorenz. Ingrid Schick, a literary agent in Munich, effected an introduction and accompanied Jonathan and myself on a visit to his home near Vienna. Lorenz was advanced in years and not in especially good health, but he was still a commanding and engaging presence. I had wanted to witness the geese following him around his estate, but it transpired that his latest passion was fish behaviour. Between two adjoining outside walls on his property he had built a large saltwater aquarium, at least three metres high and three metres across, into which he regularly climbed and, fully submerged, checked and cleaned the apparatus. Most of the time, however, he sat outside with his notebook, observing and recording the movements of the fish. We watched him for at least an hour and wondered how he could keep track of so many diverse species in such a continuous whirl of activity. But his was the kind of passionate interest in the minutiae of the natural world that characterised Durrell's enthusiasms, and it was easy to see why the two men were mutual admirers. Sadly Konrad Lorenz died before his fish studies were complete, and I have often wondered since whether anyone else will attempt such a task.

That evening in Vienna, Jonathan, Ingrid and I celebrated the success of our meeting rather too enthusiastically. The next day, before leaving for the airport, I met Jonathan for a coffee and a torte. He wasn't up for either. He looked as green as Konrad Lorenz's wellies.

'Jonathan, it's just a question of mind over matter,' I said, somewhat unhelpfully.

'If you don't shut up,' he winced, 'there's going to be matter all over the place.'

Never Negotiate with a Husky

On foreign sales trips it was better if there were two of you, or even three, to share the load and maybe work up a double act as part of a selling routine. And it was companionable after a day's business in a foreign city to sit down and share a glass while mulling over which publisher was best suited to a particular title, which would offer the better deal, which would promote it more effectively and so on. It could be a lot of fun. But if you were travelling alone, it was an altogether more challenging experience.

One winter I went solo to Norway. The snow was thick on the ground and as the taxi drove me into Oslo from the airport in the grey winter light I felt the silence of the dark woods closing in on me like a blanket. Circumstances had prevented any of the others from making the trip, and I was apprehensive about managing the dual role of presenting the books and calculating the prices correctly. Plus I was carrying six heavy art bags in addition to my own suitcase.

The first two meetings were quite promising. I walked away with an offer on the wine book, some interest in a pregnancy book, and a promise to follow up on the self-sufficiency title once there was an assurance that a section on the sousing and pickling of fish would be added to the contents (I would have to check with John Seymour – I wasn't sure that his knowledge of sousing and pickling extended beyond Elsie's pub). But now I was to meet one of the most obdurate publishers in the market, whom I will call Knut. Christopher Dorling had warned me that Dorling Kindersley had never been able to sell him a book and it would be a triumph if I succeeded.

One of the charms of central Oslo is its intimate scale. Many of the publishers are within a short distance of each other, too near to take a taxi but too far if you are lugging six art bags on foot through deep snow. My lumbering figure cast a strange shadow as I staggered the half mile toward my next destination. I was wearing a rabbit-skin coat (which had moulted embarrassingly on the previous publisher's sofa), cowboy boots, a battered trilby, and, festooned as I was with the art bags, resembled a displaced person in search of a refuge. When I finally reached the offices of Knut's Forlag I leaned in exhaustion against the front door and pressed the bell. The door opened immediately, sending me sprawling into the hallway with the art bags crashing around me. The receptionist gazed down on me with cool Nordic disdain.

'Who is it please that you wish to see?'

'Mr Knut,' I gasped, still on all fours.

'And you are?'

'Christopher Davis from Dorling Kindersley.'

'Just a moment please.'

A minute or two later the inner door opened and a huge husky came bounding out, followed by the scarecrow figure of Knut. As I moved to shake his hand, the husky lunged at the hem of my rabbit-skin coat, seized a corner in his teeth and began tugging with such ferocity that it started to rip.

'Haakon!' shouted Knut, and then said something in Norwegian which I presumed – hoped – was the equivalent of 'Drop it!' Whatever it was, Haakon paid no attention and refused to let go until he had detached a sizeable mouthful of rabbit fur.

'It's difficult, I admit,' said Knut. 'He doesn't take orders from anyone. That's why I call him Haakon. After the King, you know…'

I looked ruefully down at my mauled coat. I was hoping the dog would choke on it. As for Knut, he showed no remorse and offered no apology; he merely turned on his heel, leaving me to pick up the six bags and stagger along to his office.

As we settled down either side of his desk, Haakon installed himself underneath it with his nose on a level with my crotch and far too close to it for comfort. Every time I looked down, my gaze was met by the icy blue eyes of my tormentor. It was hard to concentrate on the job in hand. Knut offered little in the way of small talk or words of welcome. I found it difficult to make out what lay behind the austere remoteness of the person facing me. I decided to plunge in.

'We are developing a book on *Classic Wine Labels* …'

'Nej.'

'Oh. Right. How about a *Day-by-Day Pregnancy* book?'

'Nej.'

'*How to Photograph Nudes?*'

'Nej.'

'*Cooking for One?*'

'Nej. I already do. It's a lonely activity.'

He looked more morose than ever. Perhaps he shared his meals with Haakon. Maybe that was why he was so skinny.

'*Arranging Dried Flowers?*'

'Nej.'

So it went on. Nej, nej, nej to everything I pulled from my arsenal of art bags. I wasn't going to suggest the self-sufficiency book; apart from the fact that other publishers were keen on it, I didn't want Knut to offer. It would be a joyless experience if he were to publish it.

Finally, after drawing a blank on every title on the list, I threw up my hands in mock surrender and started to laugh. Was there any subject under the sun that would elicit a glimmer of interest from this Easter Island statue across the table? As I packed away the materials in the bags I decided to invent some fanciful titles. Knut had obviously had a quadruple sense-of-humour bypass and it might be fun to see if I could coax any reaction out of him.

'How about *Astrology for Dogs?*' I suggested, still busy shoving colour proofs into a bag.

'JA!'

I stopped in my tracks. I was astounded. I had to think quickly. DK hadn't even considered such a title.

'Really? Are you sure?'

'Ja. Absolutely. Haakon is a Taurus.'

'No kidding.'

'His moon is in the Seventh House, and unfortunately you come on a day when Mars is in the ascendant. How big will this book be?'

'Oh, well, er, hmm, maybe 96 pages, in a slim format. Just enough to cover all the star signs, and how they govern the behaviour of different breeds of dog.'

I was desperately treading water. I had no idea what I was talking about.

'I'd like prices for 3,000 copies and 5,000 copies,' said Knut decisively.

I pulled out my calculator. I tried to think of another title on the DK list in a similar format and to remember what it cost to manufacture.

'Well, I'll have to confirm these numbers when I get back to London, but I estimate that 3,000 copies would come in at £2.10 each...'

A throaty growl erupted under the table. Haakon's nose had moved closer to my crotch.

'...and 5,000 copies would be £2.05 each.'

Another growl. Louder and deeper. Haakon had now bared his teeth. Was this dog Knut's negotiating tool as well?

'Let's just say there may be a little room for movement on those prices' I added hastily, only too aware that there was very little room for movement between Haakon's teeth and my manhood.

'Very well' said Knut. 'I wait to hear. And to see your proposal for the book.'

A few minutes later I was out in the snowy street with

my bags and my tattered coat. Darkness had fallen and the temperature had dropped way below freezing. There wasn't a taxi in sight. I faced a long walk back to my hotel. When I get there, I thought, I'm going to treat myself to a very large whisky, even if in Norway it costs about half my monthly salary. I've carried these wretched bags the length and breadth of Oslo, Knut wasn't interested in one single item in them, he didn't even offer me a cup of coffee, his frigging hound has wrecked my overcoat, and the only title he wants to buy doesn't exist, may never exist, and I've sold it to him. How am I going to get out of that one?

But when I returned to London and recounted my adventures to Peter and Christopher, they were surprisingly upbeat.

'Knut could be right,' said Christopher. 'There might be a quirky market for such a book. We should try it out in other countries.'

Juliet Kindersley, who had come into the room carrying one of her dachshunds, was entranced by the notion.

'Ooh yes!' she said, clapping her hands. 'What a wonderful idea! We should do one for cats too.'

'Astrology for Tortoises?' I muttered wearily. 'That should be a million-seller.'

'Oh Mr Davis!' said Juliet, throwing a dog biscuit at me. 'You're just a typical Cancer. Crabby and suspicious.'

As far as this project was concerned, I accepted she was right. But I also accepted that I was probably going to have to commission it. Immediately.

In fact, we never did. The consensus was that this was not

going to make the earth move. But Knut, or the avenging spirit of his husky, may have had the last word. A few years later we were staying in the Ramada Hotel in Frankfurt, which had a swimming pool and a bar on the top floor. It was our custom to have a riotous dinner on the last night of the book fair and then repair to the pool for more drinks and, inevitably, a fair amount of horseplay. Knut was also a regular guest in the hotel and was in the habit of taking a serious swim every evening. On this occasion he was laboriously completing his quota of lengths up and down one side of the pool while the DK mob were depositing the surrounding furniture into the water. Knut was soon fighting his way through a flotilla of upturned chairs, cushions and bar stools. After a while he gave up the unequal struggle, climbed out, dried himself off and disappeared without a word. Shortly afterwards the manager appeared. The next year we found that our application for rooms at the Ramada was refused. And for the next ten years or so we were banished to a hotel in the suburb of Offenbach, far from the bright lights of the big city.

Name on the Spine

Nothing stood still at DK. Not ever. Not even for a day. Such was Peter Kindersley's restless nature there was always a new target to be achieved, a new obsession to be harnessed. It was like sharing an office with a dog that never lies down. His ambition was to control every aspect of the company's output, not just the details of a book's design but also the manner in which it was marketed and sold. As a packager we had little chance of influencing the latter to any significant degree, which could be frustrating if the publisher to whom we had sold a title did not promote it with the same loving care as we had lavished on the making of it. It was therefore only a question of time before we graduated from packager to publisher.

It happened almost by accident. Peter and I had paid a visit to the Football Association in Lancaster Gate in the hope of persuading them to produce well-designed coaching manuals with us. A predictably dull-witted meeting led nowhere. On the way back to Covent Garden in a taxi Peter asked the driver to divert to the headquarters of the Red Cross in Belgravia.

'Have you seen the *First Aid Manual*?' he asked me. 'It looks unbelievably antiquated. And yet they must sell millions of copies. It's got to be an opportunity.'

He was right. In the reception area I leafed through a dog-eared copy that looked as if it had originated in the post-war austerity years. But the printing history on the copyright page was phenomenal. How could we get to meet the right people who would see the benefits of giving their core publication a dramatic facelift?

It wasn't easy. In the first place the *First Aid Manual* was the official product of three societies – The British Red Cross Society, St John's Ambulance, and St Andrew's Ambulance Association – each of which was fronted by distinguished former military leaders of a certain grandeur, each of whom believed that their society was the first among equals. Dealing with the politics of the three bodies in itself required a master class in diplomacy, while once the deal to create a new *First Aid Manual* was eventually hammered out, there was the tricky issue of whose first aid techniques were to be represented. There was, for example, no consensus on the correct way to apply a bandage. Fortunately, we had an editor, Jemima Dunne, who was highly adept at soothing ruffled feathers and negotiating reasonable compromises. In fact, Jemima spent some 25 years at DK during which time her principal role was to keep the First Aid societies happy, and it is greatly to her credit that DK continued to win the right to publish new editions of the *First Aid Manual* throughout that period. It is the company's all-time single bestselling publication.

A visitor to 9 Henrietta Street in 1981 might have been surprised to discover the floor of one or two offices covered with inert bodies, ketchup-splashed dressings applied to different limbs. A photographer would be hovering over them. It wasn't written into anyone's contract but it soon became a fact of life that staff members, plus their partners, their children, even their pets, could at some point be corralled into modelling for DK lifestyle books. It was all part of the collective spirit of endeavour.

The first full-colour edition of the *First Aid Manual* was published in 1982. In the UK it was the first of our titles to bear the DK colophon on the spine. The logic for this was inescapable. What was the point of selling on the rights to a title to which no risk was attached and which had a guaranteed place as core stock in every bookshop? There was also the bonus of the First Aid societies ordering many thousands of copies each to supply their volunteers in the field. Thus DK became a publisher. In the first year we sold a million copies of the *Manual* in the UK alone and subsequently licensed it all over the world, adapting the contents where appropriate to suit the local first aid conventions.

The publication launch party was held in our office at the back of No 9. Everyone involved in the making of the manual crowded in, including an impressive array of military bigwigs, one of whom was General Grey. There was an awkward moment when Peter in his speech referred to him as Earl Grey, which caused some bristling ('One lump or two?' someone whispered). The overall mood, however, was one of mutual congratulation because it was a partnership that had clearly worked to the benefit of all parties.

The decision to publish the *First Aid Manual* may have been an easy one, but, having made it, there was little chance that we would continue to license other new titles to trade houses in the UK.

'We just want to do it, don't we?' was Peter's unanswerable way of proposing a collective decision, which, by his cunning use of 'we' simultaneously challenged naysayers to disagree while making them party to his course of action if they didn't. He usually reinforced his proposition by firmly gripping your elbow from behind and applying pressure with his fingers to ensure your submission was complete. It was almost impossible to have a dialogue with him on any subject once he had made

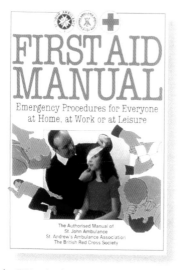

The first title to carry the DK colophon on its spine, this is also the company's all-time bestseller with more than six million copies sold.

his mind up about what he wanted to do. 'Ja, mein Führer!' was my way of reminding him that his dictatorial mindset had switched into overdrive.

The step from packager to publisher is not a small one. In those days we budgeted a new book on the basis that 35-40 per cent of the origination costs would be funded by the US, 30 per cent by the UK, and the remainder by foreign language editions. It was therefore a significant dent in the cash flow to remove the upfront UK contribution from the equation while at the same time taking on the burden of owning stock, the costs of manufacturing, marketing and distribution, the risk of the title failing, all in the cause of richer rewards to be gleaned from every copy sold. I don't know which was the greater at the time – our naivety or our bravado. Either way it's basically irrelevant. The one thing we never had was fear. If somebody tentatively raised their hand to ask, for example, 'What if none of the books reach their target?' the standard Kindersley answer was along the lines of 'Well, it will be interesting, and besides we'll learn a lot along the way. But it won't be the end of the world.' In this respect he was at his most inspiring and it was impossible not to feel exhilarated that he had invited you to join him on the next adventure.

The new DK publishing imprint was launched in the autumn of 1982. Besides the *First Aid Manual* and another title published with the three societies, *Caring for the Sick*, it included *The Guitar Handbook* (published in hardback simultaneously with a Pan paperback edition), *The Sweater Book* (another Amy Carroll production) and a bizarre solve-it-yourself detective book, *Crime and Puzzlement*. The UK publishing operation was headed by Ian Grant, who had previously co-run a small imprint called Ash & Grant, which DK had taken over and used to launch a handful of titles via WHS Distributors. (WHSD was itself run by Duncan Baird and Frank Wintle. The latter subsequently found greater fame as Edward Rutherfurd, the author of a line of door-stopping historical sagas.) DK's sales and distribution were handled by our neighbours five doors away down Henrietta Street, Victor Gollancz, under the benign guidance of Nigel Sisson.

We didn't publish everything we produced in those early years of the imprint – the continuing list of photography titles was mostly licensed to Ebury who had marketed the first books so successfully. But we gradually added core reference to our UK backlist, including two Miriam Stoppard titles in 1983 – *The Baby Care Book* and *The 50 Plus Lifeguide* – and a third, *The Pregnancy and Birth Book*, the following year. And *The Garden Book* by John Brookes, a title funded by an advance commission from the EBG, one of the giant thriving branches of the Bertelsmann book clubs in Germany, who took 200,000 copies as a main selection, rapidly established itself as an ideal model of a DK book – a frontlist hit sold in multiple languages that evolved into a reprinting backlist staple.

It was clear that the VG reps enjoyed the extra incentive of selling attractively designed how-to manuals alongside the worthy but comparatively sombre offerings from their own house. Inevitably they soon wanted more titles than we could produce, which forced us into a period of self-examination. What were our priorities? Were we a packager or a publisher?

The number of titles we packaged was based on what we could create and sell to publishers around the world in any given year. The more titles we created, the more we had to recruit the staff to make them. Every book was labour-intensive and editors and designers could only work full-time on one title at a time. There wasn't necessarily a problem in growing this way because, in theory at least, the packaged titles would be self-funding. But once you start publishing in your home market, the whole infrastructure needed to publicise, promote and distribute the list demands a level of turnover to support it, and the building of a list needs a level of visibility that can only be garnered by a recognisable volume.

It was a dilemma and, in trying to resolve it, our inexperience led us down a path that, in retrospect, was perhaps misguided. We thought we could boost our UK turnover, and our profits, by adding a line of traditional trade books to our home-grown output. We also believed that if we could attract name authors to this list then we could earn a cachet of respectability in the UK publishing milieu. (As one grande dame of the business once said to me at a dinner, 'Well, DK doesn't count as a publisher – you're below the salt' – though I have to say this social ranking was not uppermost in our minds as we had nothing but contempt for that kind of unreconstructed snobbery.)

It came to my attention at this time that Jill Norman, formerly the revered queen of cookery publishing at Penguin and beloved by many authors, was now languishing at Robert Hale. We invited her to create a UK list for us in parallel with our illustrated titles on food and wine, which she duly did, bringing in Elizabeth David, whose classic cookbooks we republished in enhanced hardback editions, Richard Olney, Frances Bissell, Julie Sahni, Paula Wolfert and, introducing to the UK for the first time, the American wine guru, Robert Parker. This was a distinguished crop of names by any measure, but alas our expectations were not matched by the sales and therein lay one of the first lessons of publishing. A list known for its distinctive design characteristics, such as DK was beginning to develop, does not mix with a traditional unillustrated style of publishing. Even though the VG reps had been used to selling the latter, once they had DK books in their bag they expected – and they led their customers to expect – that any book with the DK colophon on the spine should live up to the illustrated standards associated with it. Years later, when Penguin took over DK and assigned the list to their own sales force rather than retaining the unique dedication and commitment of the sales team that had served us so well for years, the truth of this mismatch came home even more strongly.

Naturally, it was a disappointment to us, and especially to Jill, that the experiment had to be curtailed after a few years, but maybe she had some consolation in that she converted to become a successful DK author herself. In any event, by the time this happened, our annual output had expanded to the point where our UK turnover exceeded VG's and we were ready to break away with our own team of reps. Jill would certainly have found it ironic that one of the bestselling DK titles of the mid-1980s was a cookbook, not from the pen of one of her Olympian luminaries, but from Sarah Brown, a former Scarborough showgirl who was now fronting the first populist BBC series on vegetarian cooking. We gave her book the full DK treatment but, however enticingly we tried to photograph the dishes, there was no escaping the fact that the food was uniformly brown. And somewhat heavy looking. And nearly all the vegetables were diced. Sarah was a whizz at dicing. But the title was a huge hit, and we commissioned more from her.

The second Sarah Brown title, *The Healthy Living Cookbook*, was launched at a lunch for the assembled trade luminaries at the BA conference in Eastbourne. Alas, the hotel chef had misread the recipe for the soup and apparently quadrupled the specified amount of salt. After the introductory speeches, the guests raised the spoons to their lips and immediately reached for their wine glasses. The spoons refused to sink into the soup but lay on the surface. The one benefit of the Dead Sea Soup episode was that everyone drank so much they couldn't remember it.

Hughes the Money

It was often hard to know, at the beginning of a publisher-author relationship, how it would develop. Sometimes it remained strictly functional – write, deliver, edit, exit. At the opposite extreme, it became involving to a degree whereby the manuscript was submitted along with a carousel full of the emotional baggage of an unfulfilled life. Somehow an editor, as midwife to the birth of a book, has to steer a middle course that engages the trust of an author without allowing his or her own life to be swamped by a tidal wave of the writer's insecurities or crushed by preening egotism. The profession of editor, like that of a midwife, is in theory at least among the most self-effacing of callings, but the role requires one to be prepared to deal with a thousand natural shocks along the rocky road from the conception of a book to its final execution. An author who is emotionally demanding is the most exhausting, and an author who ignores every deadline is the most frustrating, but when the chemistry between editor and writer is right and brings forth fruitfulness, it can be one of the most rewarding jobs in the world. Memory tends to bury the dark episodes but hangs on to the sunnier ones, especially those with a comical side.

When John Seymour's *Complete Book of Self-Sufficiency* became a bestseller in Germany, he was regarded as a folk hero across that country. With the publication of the follow up, *The Self-Sufficient Gardener*, he acquired the status of a cult figure and Ravensburger, the German publisher, decided it was time to celebrate this success with a massive knees-up during the Frankfurt Book Fair. It was to be held in some bogus mock-Tudor farmhouse several miles outside the city. John had never been to Frankfurt before but he somehow managed to escape the clutches of his minders, before we set out for the party. We assumed he must have been offered a lift by one of the Ravensburger team. Not so. As we drove down the autobahn in the dark and the teeming rain, there along the hard shoulder was the unmistakable figure of Mr Seymour trudging hopefully in an easterly direction as giant articulated trucks hurtled past and doused him with their spray. We pulled over in front of him.

'John, what on earth are you doing? It's miles from here.'

'Oh, is it? I asked a friendly cab driver and he pointed me in this direction. Said it wasn't far.'

He climbed into the back of the car smelling of wet dog. As we entered the giant barn at the farmhouse, which had been converted into a bierkeller for the night but with the added trappings of home-baked bread, home-made sausages und so weiter, the assembled throng of German publishers, booksellers and assorted groupies rose as one to hail their bedraggled hero like a rock star. Poor John. It wasn't his scene. He was desperate for a quiet beaker of ale. Before he could even swallow a draft, he was summoned to the stage by his host, the ersatz farmer.

'Herr Seymour, bitte, over here please. We must ask you to perform us a small ceremony in honour of our guests tonight.'

On the stage was a large tethered goat with a bucket and stool beside it.

'Please Herr Seymour, you will be so kind as to fill this bucket with some of the goat milch for everyone to taste and know how wonderful it is to have your own animal and to drink its milch direct from the bosom.'

John groaned.

'You really want me to do this?'

'Ja, ja, it will be of the utmost honour for our special occasion to celebrate your fantastic books about the joys of self-sufficiency. Please, if you will, over here.'

John stomped across the stage in his muddy boots and perched on the stool beside the goat. The room fell silent. As his fingers squeezed the teats and the first jets of warm milk zinged into the bucket, the barn echoed to ecstatic cheers. He might have been the Pope blessing the throng in St Peter's Square.

A few minutes later he held up the bucket.

'Who wants to sample this?' he asked.

Hundreds of hands shot up, as if he had thrown a football shirt into the crowd. The bucket was passed around, tipped back and handed along until it was empty. John came back to our table.

'Goats!' he said. 'I can't abide 'em. And as for goat's milk, give me a beer any day.'

Several hours later, when we had supped our fill, he and I hitched a lift with the Ravensburger publicity woman, squatting in the back of her van.

'Christopher,' he confided, 'I've got a few problems down at my own farm. I may need your help. I'll drop you a line when I get home.'

I could guess what was coming. Although the two self-sufficiency books had racked up large numbers worldwide, there always seemed to be a gap between what the royalties delivered and what John needed to keep his smallholding going. It was a mystery where the money went, although I suspected that the old boy was preyed on by a number of human parasites who contributed little to the enterprise yet benefited from his bountiful good nature. Sure enough, a pleading letter from John arrived (mud speckled as usual) asking me if I would mind accompanying him on a visit to his local bank, to impress upon the manager that there was indeed a crock of gold waiting just around the corner.

I cobbled together as rosy a picture as I could paint of John's future earnings, plus a commitment to publish another book, and drove to West Wales. Furthermore, in an effort to confer on Hughes the Money, as John called the bank manager, an impression of my publishing seniority and gravitas, I had had a haircut and was relatively smartly dressed in a suit and tie.

Unfortunately, when I arrived at the farm, John was in a

distant field forking out hay from a wagon.

'Must get this finished while the weather holds!' he shouted. 'Come and give us a hand so we can get it done quicker.'

There was no option if we were going to make the appointment at the bank, so I set off across the field, realising too late that it was a quagmire liberally mined with cowpats. When we finally presented ourselves in the office of Mr Hughes, it was not a convincing spectacle. Both of us had wisps of hay attached to our clothing and hair, and my black loafers were daubed with mud and dung.

'Publisher is it, are you, Mr Davis?' said Hughes the Money, giving me a quizzical once over. 'Looks to me like you're working on the farm and John here has dressed you up in Sunday Bible black to impress me.'

I tightened the knot in my tie and pulled at my shirt cuffs.

'I can assure you, Mr Hughes, that I am John's publisher and the only work I have done on the farm was in the past hour which accounts for my relatively dishevelled appearance.'

Hughes the Money looked unconvinced until I brought out the document I had compiled, listing the rights sold around the world and John's predicted future royalties. While this was accurate at its baseline, I had embellished the earnings with a flourish of optimism. If his books had been such huge bestsellers in Germany, who was to say that they wouldn't hit the heights in other European markets?

'So you think the book will sell 10,000 copies in Lithuania, do you, Mr Davis? Oh, and in Estonia too. Good heavens, and in Latvia, and the Ukraine!'

'Well, we have an agency in Eastern Europe which is achieving remarkable sales for us,' I said. 'These markets are hungry for practical books at affordable prices.'

'But first they have to translate the book, yes?' said Hughes. 'Then they have to publish it. Then it has to be a success. And then they submit royalties after six months. It's a very drawn-out process, if I understand it correctly, Mr Davis, and therefore these monies might not be reaching John's account until at least two years from now. Am I right, look you?'

'Yes, but we will receive an advance on those royalties, and there will be other royalties coming in from the countries that have already published John's books,' I countered. 'There's no sign of a drop off in sales yet. And furthermore,' I added, flourishing a contract in front of the bank manager, 'here is an agreement for another title. And we can pay a decent advance on signature of this.'

Hughes looked marginally less sceptical, but John was shifting uncomfortably in his seat.

'I've got a pressing problem' he said, 'that needs solving today. Or not later than tomorrow. My suppliers are banging on the door and threatening to cut me off or bring in the bailiffs if I don't come up with at least an interim payment. You can see that we should have a healthy balance over the coming year or two, but the way things are going at the moment, I'm not going to be able to spare the time to even start the next book.'

'Yes, John, but with respect I've heard this many times before from you,' said Hughes. 'It's always jam tomorrow. But at the moment you don't even have bread to put it on, let alone butter.'

This wasn't going well. I looked out of the window at the dismal scene – Welsh rain falling like stair rods onto slate roofs, the town closed in on itself like a waterlogged hedgehog. There wasn't going to be an outburst of generosity from Hughes the Money.

Eventually a meagre extension to John's overdraft was conceded. John suggested we repair to Elsie's pub.

'Trouble is, Christopher,' said John, lowering a pint in a couple of gulps, 'that only gives me a very temporary breather. I need a few hundred more to stave off the barbarians at the gate.'

'OK, I'll make up the difference,' I said, taking out my chequebook. 'I'll sort this out at the office, but it will have to come out of your next royalty statement.'

'Good man,' said John. 'It will turn out all right in the end, you'll see. Two more pints please, Elsie. And one for yourself.'

I should have guessed it wasn't going to end there. One pint followed another and soon Elsie's tiny hostelry was heaving with thirsty Welshmen, the word having spread through the lanes and hedgerows that John Seymour was buying. I watched as my loan ebbed away down their throats and leaked into the urinals, but John was oblivious. Never a man to let even the sniff of a good party get away, he was now conducting the singing. Through the long afternoon and into the evening the damp valley echoed to the ribald choir, and by the time darkness fell I knew that I was in no state to attempt the drive to London.

Together we staggered back to the farm. John showed me up to a sparsely furnished room in a primitive outhouse. For some unexplained reason, an old leg of lamb was hanging from a rafter above the washbasin. In the dim light cast by a fly-coated low wattage bulb, I could detect that the room was well populated with miscellaneous wildlife.

'I'm afraid you'll have to kip in here, old boy,' said John. 'It's clean enough. Here's a tarpaulin in case the rain drips through the roof.'

I went out onto the landing. There was an ancient pay phone on the wall. I fumbled around in my pockets for the right coins.

'Linda, it's me,' I slurred. 'I can't get back tonight.'

'God, you sound wrecked. Where the hell are you?'

'I'm in an outhouse. In Wales. In the rain. In the dark. There are things snuffling and scuttling about, you know, creatures of the night, but I don't know what they are or where they are…. Oh shit, something's crawling up my leg…'

I belched into the phone. There was an exasperated sigh at the other end. Then the line went dead.

Revolution on the Page

All trade publishers, with the exception of the most sedentary imprints, thrive on opportunism. Like predatory creatures watching for a flicker of movement in the undergrowth, they hunt for the first signs of a new trend emerging in the zeitgeist and pounce on it. Dorling Kindersley was no exception. We had ridden the waves of public interest in photography, self-sufficiency, house plants, garden design, vegetarian food, and even the knitting of designer sweaters. Now, in 1983, the New New Thing was the rise and rise of the personal computer.

As more and more people clamoured to master the RAMs and ROMs of the new technology on their desk and sought guidance on how to choose and use the microcomputer that would best serve their purpose, a floodgate of publishing opportunity was opened. Most of the titles produced were text-based manuals. At DK we sought to achieve a point of difference by creating step-by-step programming courses illustrated with photographs of the relevant screen displays.

Each title in the *Screen-Shot Programming* series was dedicated to a specific brand of computer and covered such long-forgotten gems as the BBC Micro, the Sinclair ZX Spectrum, the Commodore 64, the Acorn Electron, the Apple IIc and the Apple IIe. (We even, in the white heat of this new revolution, ventured briefly into software, launching an imprint called GOLDSTAR, which was slated to cover Entertainment, Education and Home Reference. 'Have you got what it takes to become the Supreme Galactic Adventurer?' was one of the tease lines in the catalogue.)

The culmination of the programme was a commission from Sinclair Research to create the *ZX Spectrum+ User Guide*, a full-colour manual to be packaged in the carton with this new computer. The challenge facing the creative team and the production department was that this order had to be fulfilled in six weeks and produced in nineteen languages simultaneously. But with an initial print run of 750,000 copies, it was a bait we were prepared to swallow, and we duly delivered. Just in time, it transpired, as this was at the tail end of the computer books boom, which subsided as rapidly as it had risen. The DK catalogue for 1986 boasts a range of computer titles that totalled more than two million copies in print. In the 1987 catalogue the category doesn't even exist.

We were lucky. We might even have been smart. We got in early, we sold a lot of books, and we got out in time, without the penalty of heavy inventory on our hands. We also expanded into the comparatively luxurious offices next door which had, coincidentally, been occupied by Acorn. But the real long-term benefit to the company was the acquired knowledge of how computers work, and, even more significantly, how we could use that knowledge to good effect in creating our own books. For editors and designers the Apple Mac quickly became the favoured medium. The skirting boards of the offices disappeared behind a spaghetti of cabling, and seemingly every week cartons bearing the distinctive Apple logo piled up in reception, as a new project got under way and demanded the latest kit. It was said that for many years DK was Apple's single largest account in the UK. Gone were messy paste-ups and the brief hits enjoyed from the inhalation of cow gum; gone were two-colour artworks and clunky cutaway diagrams. Now the screen opened onto a pure white field on which could be planted a full-colour photographic cut-out image, moved here and there to accommodate text, dotted with leader lines like acupuncture needles to highlight its features, and then given a three-dimensional twist by the subtle addition of a shadow. It was a revolution, one that led directly from our early embrace of the computer as a book-making tool.

DK's subsequent reputation as a cutting-edge producer of illustrated reference rests largely on that particular look – the cut-out images on a white background. But it didn't become a signature style until the launch of the *Eyewitness* books in 1988, fourteen years after the company's founding. In the first ten years we had produced exactly 100 titles. While they all achieved a level of complexity in the page design, they all used artworks as the means of explaining process, usually in two colours, and where photographs were deployed, these were generally squared up or full-page bleeds. There were just two exceptions – *The Book of Ingredients* (1980) and *The Amateur*

Naturalist (1982) – where the device of cut-out photography was the key feature. Looking back, it is surprising that we did not seize on that style and build on it more quickly.

In 1985 one title – *Stretch & Relax* (so-called because the US market thought Yoga too esoteric) – featured annotated photographs of the asanas, and in 1986 one title – *The Complete Book of Dried Flowers* – included stunning cut-out displays. Both titles performed brilliantly, especially *Dried Flowers*, which sold out so fast in the UK that we had to airfreight books from Hong Kong at vast expense to meet the demand. Was this title a bestseller because it was another example of a book satisfying public interest just as the wave was peaking? Or was it because of the brilliance of Malcolm Hillier and Colin Hilton's arrangements? Or was it because the

The overhead photography featured in *The Book of Ingredients* and *The Amateur Naturalist*, right, inspired Pierre Marchand of Gallimard to approach DK with the idea of creating the Eyewitness series.

DK photographic treatment was so much more compelling than the competing books on the subject? Well, the answer is probably yes to all three questions. But, as far as the design style goes, it was still the exception rather than the rule and maybe we hadn't yet realised how potent it could be.

It was a phone call from Pierre Marchand at Gallimard that changed everything. Christine Baker was also on the line to bridge the gap between my schoolboy French and Pierre's reluctant English.

' 'Allo, Christophe, bonjour.'

'Bonjour, Pierre, ça va?'

'Oui, oui, très bien, merci. Alors, vous connaissez cette livre des *Ingredients du Cuisine*?'

'Oui, naturellement.'

'Bon. J'aime beaucoup la style photographique là-dedans. C'est comme un musée gastronomique. Alors, j'ai une idée nouvelle. C'est à prendre des photographies comme ça pour beaucoup des objets du monde.'

'Comment?' (What is he talking about?)

'Et après a faire une librairie – vingt-quatre, trente-six, quarante-huit titres…. Une grande idée. Fantastique…'

'Christine, you have to help me here. Please explain a bit more.'

'Pierre is a great admirer of the photographic style you used in *The Book of Ingredients* and in *The Amateur Naturalist*. He believes you can use this style to capture almost any subject and we could together produce an amazing series of information books for children.'

'Can you give me an example of what he is thinking about?'

'Well, if you take a subject like Mountain, you could make cut-out photographs of all the equipment you need to climb – crampons, gloves, goggles, etc – then of the different rock formations, of the plants and flowers and wildlife, of the food supplies you need, of weather, snow and ice, cloud formations, glaciers….'

'OK, I'm beginning to get the picture. I'm sure we would be interested to hear more. Can we meet to get a clearer idea what he is thinking about?'

So it began. I didn't really have a picture at all. I relayed this to Peter and to Alan Buckingham, who seemed the candidate best suited to take on such an assignment. Pierre and Christine came over to London and we met in the windowless gloom of

The Bunker at 9 Henrietta Street. Gradually the fog cleared. You could select Bird as a topic, photograph different species, their plumage, skeletons, wings, feathers, beaks, feet, nests, everything that makes a bird a bird. But would that really constitute an appealing book? We were still sceptical, and a little bewildered, when the meeting was over.

Now I look back on the eighteen months following that meeting as the most stimulating and enjoyable of my time in the company. It was a genuine collaboration between two of the most creative forces in publishing – Pierre Marchand, the passionate Breton, who had transformed Gallimard Jeunesse into a world leader in juvenile books, and Peter Kindersley, who was driving DK into a dominating position in illustrated reference. They had no common language and really no common interests, except the endless desire for beauty and excellence in their books. But each had a coterie to smooth communications. Gallimard had use of a boat, leased to them by Renault, which was moored on the Seine in the shadow of Notre Dame, and there we would meet – Pierre with his team of elegant, competent women (Hedwige Pasquet, Christine Baker et al), Peter with his bearded ruffians (Alan, myself) and Annie Frankland, the French-born DK rights manager. A trip to Paris, lunch on the Seine, the exchange of ideas, the oxygen of inventing the new – a working life that dreams are built on. But it was real work. Gradually the pages took shape. We submitted our layouts of photographic images in all their Calvinist purity. Pierre, who doodled endlessly on a pad, would frown and then deliver the Gallic romantic touch – the addition of small drawings or an engraving, dropped in to give a human dimension to the page. Pristine elegance and decorative panache – it was a perfect marriage.

After months of experimentation with the content, and likewise months of discussion about what form a contract between Gallimard and DK would take, it was concluded that a joint venture between the two companies was the most appropriate. DK would, with creative input from Gallimard, produce, print and sell the series round the world and the net proceeds would be split. Pierre Marchand was confident that we had struck on a winning formula; we were less sure, mainly because our exposure to the world of children's books had been so limited. In the first twelve years of the company's life we had produced just three titles aimed at children – *The Origin of Johnny* (the first of all); *Hedgerow*, the illustrated story of the life of one hedge from Saxon times to the bulldozing destruction of the present day; and *Being Born*. We had not ventured further into this market in the mistaken belief that there wouldn't be enough margin to justify our doing so.

A visit by Peter Kindersley and Ruth Sandys, the international sales director, to Bologna in the mid '80s had changed this view. They could see there was a gap in the market for information books for the young. We had therefore begun work on a series of artwork-based titles called *Windows on the World*, which received a positive response at the following Bologna and was launched in 1987. Six popular topics – *Human Body*, *Dinosaurs*, *Planets*, *Animals*, *Life Through the Ages*, and *Wonders of the World* – were given fresh appeal by quality illustrators and imaginative design. The international markets bought into the series and a first printing of more than 250,000 copies confirmed that this was an area of the bookshop we had unjustly neglected.

There wasn't any ambiguity about the concept of *Windows on the World* or its target audience. But the Gallimard/DK project – now christened *Eyewitness* (for which I claim a modest credit) – was something else. Nobody had ever seen anything like it. We canvassed opinion.

'Sixty-four pages of hardback non-fiction at £6.95? You won't be able to give it away,' was the verdict of one UK children's publisher.

As we carted the sample pages of the first volumes around New York, we met the same stonewalling dismissal. Children's publishing was then all about novelties and picture books. Every single publisher turned it down until at last Janet Schulman at Knopf recognised the spark of something different. She wasn't sure but she was prepared to give it a shot. Frankfurt in 1987 confirmed her faith, and bolstered ours. By then we had proofs of the launch titles – *Bird*, *Rock & Mineral*, *Skeleton* and *Arms & Armour* – and the displays on the stand became a focal point of the book fair. The response was sensational – publishers from all corners of the globe clamoured for a piece of the action. Here was a series that not only broke the mould in terms of its presentation, it also delivered cross-generational appeal. When asked for the age level it was supposed to address, our stock response was 7–77.

Eyewitness struck another chord, which the New York publishers hadn't foreseen. Their recent concentration on picture books and novelties wasn't sufficient to satisfy the multitude of baby boomers desperate for their kids to have quality information books in the home to give them a better chance of succeeding at school. This area of the market had somehow been ignored for years, and such titles as did exist were usually terminally unappealing.

The advantage that we had created for ourselves at DK was equivalent to seeking members to join an exclusive club. We were out on our own because we had also broken the rules of children's publishing in terms of cost. Every page of an *Eyewitness* book cost £1,000 to originate; a budget of £60,000 per title was probably ten times what a traditional publisher would have spent on an information book of 64 pages. This didn't provoke disbelief, it provoked desire. And the economies of scale from printing so many co-editions made it possible. A publisher in, say, Denmark could therefore acquire for his list a title that he couldn't possibly have created himself, at a price that he couldn't have achieved if he had printed on his own, and could launch it at a retail price in his own market equivalent to other 64-page information books but with palpably more quality than the competition. This formula worked around the world, and *Eyewitness* became a phenomenon. Within a year of publishing the first tranche of titles, we had sold one million copies. The series has since extended to more than 120 titles and racked up sales of more than 50 million in 40 languages.

While the early breakthrough success of *Eyewitness* meant that DK could henceforth develop a children's publishing strand in parallel with adult books, it conferred another benefit that was equally transformational – the company-wide feeling that we could make an interesting book on almost any subject, especially if we could photograph it in that signature style. This notion became encapsulated in an oft-repeated mantra: 'There's no such thing as a boring subject, only boring ways of presenting it'. Everyone involved in *Eyewitness* became enthused by the possibilities of what we could achieve and aware of the graphic potential of everyday objects on a page. A favourite topic of Peter Kindersley was to demonstrate how a can of Coke, crushed in the gutter, looks like nothing more than it is – a crushed can of Coke – but if you lift it, place it on a white background, photograph it and maybe highlight its features, with a shadow dropped beside it, then it becomes an object of interest. Thus, like Warhol's soup cans, the commonplace acquires charisma.

Near the Gallimard offices in the Rue du Bac in Paris there was a shop full of skeletons, of all sorts. After our meetings with Pierre Marchand, we would enter its ghostly interior and buy what we could easily carry back to London. As *Skeleton* was one of the first *Eyewitness* titles, we needed to source the contents wherever we could. Subsequently, we entered into an agreement with the Natural History Museum whereby they would collaborate and approve the content of nature titles, while we were given licence to ransack their archives. This proved to be a treasure chest – every drawer, cabinet and cupboard in the depths of that great building yielded a cascade of bones, innumerable skulls from the grazing antelope of the Serengeti brought back as trophies by the Great White Hunters of the Victorian age, skeletons of birds, bats, frogs, moles, dogs, cats, horses, monkeys, snakes, the jaw of a shark, the flipper of a seal, the leg of an ostrich, the perfectly preserved bone structure of a cod…

The *Eyewitness* "look" created a revolution in juvenile non-fiction when the first titles were launched in 1988. The series became a phenomenon, selling more than 50 million copies.

Once the use of cut-out photography against a white background had been established as a hallmark of DK design, there seemed no limit to what could be achieved. The business of photographing all manner of wildlife in the studio could be difficult, even dangerous, but was ultimately rewarding for the immediacy and clarity of the effect.

Skulls and bones were relatively easy to photograph. We also needed the living flesh and blood of the creatures themselves, not against the background of their natural habitat but, again, photographed in cut-out isolation. For this we usually had to arrange for the animals to be brought to the studio we had set up in Earlham Street. Over the years a succession of large and frequently dangerous creatures were cajoled, nudged, pushed or enticed into a spacious white-walled room where, under the watchful eye of the keeper and the anxious eye of the photographer, they were persuaded to remain still long enough to be captured on film. Where the more unpredictable species, such as the big cats, were concerned, the photographer was usually in a cage in the centre of the studio while the lion or tiger roamed the space in front of a giant white sheet. The making of books had turned into a challenging, exciting, vivid, hilarious and occasionally hazardous adventure. But everyone involved, whether editing, designing, researching, selling or managing, would surely say it was the best of times.

Impressionists in the Men's Room

It is an experience universally acknowledged that a creative company, beginning as it usually does with high ideals and limitless horizons, will sooner or later face the growing pains that accompany success. The staff expands, a structural hierarchy gets imposed, the status of job titles becomes an issue, bigger premises are required and have to be managed, more sophisticated accounting systems are needed to match the company's expansion, bureaucracy creeps in, and so forth.

We were not trained business managers. Basically, we were a bunch of (mostly) editors and designers who had hit on a winning formula. As Peter said to me years later: 'We were good at starting a company but not so good at running it.' I would agree with him up to a point, yet there is also much to be said for a company driven by the passion and foresight of a creative genius, however eccentrically he behaves and however contradictory his messages to the staff, rather than a suited professional from the detached world of commerce. On the other hand, the pact that Peter and I jokily enjoyed of never hiring "grown-ups" was probably taken too literally for too long.

We were, for example, always one accountant behind the gain line. The first did a runner, leaving a bunch of uncashed cheques in his desk drawer, when he realised the job was beyond him. The second, Robin Hayfield, was a delightful person to work with in the context of a small cottage industry. A genuine alternative to the conventional image of accountancy, he was a bearded vegan who wore a sweater, thick socks and bungee shoes and filed the accounts with a pencil. But by the time he left, to follow his true star and become a homeopath, Dorling Kindersley had a staff of 100 and a turnover of £10 million. We had expanded into three other buildings in Henrietta Street and had also opened an office in Richmond, a creative outpost run by Roger Bristow and Jackie Douglas. We were also in the process of establishing our own German rights business in Stuttgart. Life was becoming complicated. It needed more than a pencil and a pocket calculator.

There had always been some friction between Christopher Dorling and Caroline Oakes on the one side, and Peter Kindersley on the other, about the levels of professional support the company needed. In the early days the audited accounts were handled by a small firm in Kingston, amiably run by a man straight off a Happy Families card called Bill Ledger. Likewise legal matters were referred on an ad hoc basis to a friendly solicitor. Then Peter, in one of his ruthless streaks, demanded that we dispense with these inexpensive providers and switch to top-dollar City firms – Binder Hamlyn for the auditing and Herbert Smith for legal advice. He was probably pressed into the latter by one of his smooth-talking Kennington neighbours. Christopher and Caroline didn't think the fees justified the change; Peter was adamant. He went ahead.

Around the same time it was decided that DK needed a managing director. It was certainly required for the business, and was probably also necessary for the staff who had never been quite sure where the decision making lay at the top of the company. From the ensuing headhunt Richard Harman emerged as the winner, and he joined our senior quartet in the back office of No 9.

The quartet didn't last for long. It was becoming increasingly clear as the company expanded that the management styles of Christopher and Peter were less compatible than they had been at the start. It seemed to me that Christopher found it harder to deal with Peter as time went by – Caroline certainly did – and was probably frustrated by the realisation that his views on a subject, if not in accord with Peter's, would be disregarded. Thus one of Richard Harman's tasks was to help engineer Christopher and Caroline's wish for a graceful and appropriately rewarded exit. In the autumn of 1987 they departed to a handsome house in Sussex where Christopher indulged his hobbies of forestry and oil painting and Caroline opened an alternative therapy centre. To this day they have not publicly expressed any regret at their decision, which says much for the serenity of spirit their country life has given them.

For those of us who had been with the outfit from the beginning it was sad to see them leave. We had been pioneers together in that VW camper van bucketing down the autobahn to Frankfurt. And both of them had consistently stood for the "human factor" in the company. Now, the business had evolved and, with the advent of Richard, a more professional note was being sounded. It needed to be because the search was on to find the candidate to take on Christopher's 50 per cent stake. More critically, it was to find the candidate who would be prepared to eyeball Peter Kindersley on an equal footing – at least as difficult a task as finding a wife to satisfy Henry VIII.

A solution was eventually engineered by the amiable goodwill of John Pope. John had been instrumental in commissioning DK to create *Success with Houseplants* for Reader's Digest back in the late '70s. Since then the US office of RD had benefited considerably from their mailings of other DK titles – *American Medical Association Family Medical Guide*, *American Medical Association Encyclopedia of Medicine*, *American Medical Association Guide to Drugs*, *Good Housekeeping Step-by-Step Cookbook* – and the prospect of a continuing partnership was attractive to us as they could bring such significant quantities to supplement any trade sales of our major titles. There were also personal relationships on several levels between the companies, but especially between John and his wife Anne, and Peter and Juliet Kindersley.

From a business point of view the prospect of a partnership between RD and DK looked to tick most of the boxes. Peter could see that. But he could also see, as could those of us who knew the Digest relatively well, that there were likely to be incompatibilities in the two companies' cultures. RD was an amazingly effective sales machine, but the process to which it subjected itself en route to publishing a title was tortuous in the extreme. They only produced about six titles a year for their main selections, and each one had to go through multiple layers of testing before it was commissioned. While this ensured that each title was pitched perfectly to the readership it addressed, it was slow, cumbersome and conservative, the very characteristics which came to dominate their culture. We were used to this. Every Frankfurt a cohort of Digest outriders from their various offices around the globe would descend en masse onto our stand. In that cramped space it took ten minutes to arrange for everyone to be seated, served with coffee, and generally introduced over pleasantries about the state of the market, recent successes, etc, etc. In the limited time available before they had to disperse to other meetings, we would unveil our major forthcoming book ideas one by one. They would nod and make notes, criticise the content in a nitpicking way – seeing the small picture but not the big one – and, finally, by the end of the meeting decide that it would possibly be worth Q-testing one or two of the projects in particular markets. You knew that it would then take months to organise a Q-test, months to get a result, and if by some chance this proved positive, more months would go by before they would decide to commission a brochure for further market testing. If the subject had any topical validity it was likely to have evaporated by the time the book appeared. The ultimate prize of a massive mailing was worth a great deal, but with the majority of our titles we just had to get on and produce them.

There were exceptions. The Australian and Canadian offices of RD, in which Robert Sarsfield and Loraine Taylor were key operators, were more entrepreneurial and could buy for trade and catalogue sales without going through the long testing procedures. The French likewise. But we knew that if RD was going to own half of DK, it would be the conservative elements at its heart we would have to assuage. Or not.

The early signs, after the deal was struck, were not encouraging. The UK branch of the Digest was clearly unhappy that the liaison had taken place at all, while some of the senior US personnel who visited the DK offices, expressed surprise that it had happened and wondered at the logic of it.

'We haven't bought them to make money, that's for sure,' was the contemptuous verdict of one veteran.

For DK there were advantages. Our amateur management methods were straightened out somewhat, the financial reporting smartened up, and we were forced into looking at the business in a more strategic long-term light. These cosmetic improvements, however, did not disguise the discomfort we felt at dealing with RD as a partner. Nowhere was the contrast more marked than in the differing atmospheres of the two head offices. The rambling warrens of the buildings in Covent Garden were chaotic, untidy, informal, constantly shifting but constantly inspiring. They were alive with possibilities and creative endeavour. When we visited Pleasantville in upstate New York, on the other hand, we discovered that it was laid out like a college campus and was a strange mixture of sophistication and white-bread ordinariness. The reception area and corridors were lined with the remarkable collection of Impressionist and Post-Impressionist paintings accumulated by the founding Wallis family. There was even a Sisley in the men's room. But there was little sign of human activity, and the only movement in the main courtyard came from a small robot, which hummed down the pathway as it conveyed the internal mail from one building to another. In the bedrooms allocated to guests there was a copy of the Gideon Bible and a handful of RD condensed books. To me this gloomy austerity brought back memories of my first night at boarding school.

It only took a few months for Peter Kindersley's restless spirit to kick in and start striking sparks off his American counterparts. What began as a vociferous exchange of ideas predictably deteriorated into generalised insults hurled at the entire Digest emporium. His frustration was understandable, but the tactic of abuse won him no favours. John Pope, ever genial, ever conciliatory, did his best to douse Peter's flames and intercede on his behalf with his Digest colleagues, but he probably knew that it was going to be an unwinnable war. The Digest rightly had a reputation as an excellent employer. It took very good care of its people, the benefits were generous, and the atmosphere was collegiate. They had an unwritten code of honour that anything stated by outside parties about their business or their people would be openly reported to all the senior managers. Thus Peter's scattergun volleys of contempt were assiduously assembled into an arsenal of evidence with which to confront him. He was not contrite.

Maybe the partnership would have worked better at an

earlier point in DK's evolution. The timing was wrong. Six months after RD acquired Christopher's stake, we launched the *Eyewitness* books. From that moment, in the spring of 1988, we were fired up by the limitless vistas engendered by that breakthrough style of design. We wanted to expand, and quickly. We wanted investment, and the support and backing of a large, safe organisation. We wanted RD to become our principal customer. We knew instinctively that they needed us – their franchise of 50-plus white conservative males in rural America was ageing and declining. We felt they should be moving into juvenile books, and addressing the younger wannabe end of the adult market too. When they turned down the chance to acquire the US rights to the *Eyewitness* series, we realised that we were operating in a parallel but essentially incompatible universe. I remember saying to Peter, in a jesting, throwaway remark, that attempting to persuade RD to buy into our ideas was like trying to push a dinosaur through a cat flap. He, of course, repeated this to one of their management team, and my name was added to their black book.

Mammoth Sales

The German book market is a large and complex beast. Unlike most of the major book-buying markets of the world, its publishing centres are not confined to one or two cities but sprinkled across the face of the country like a rash. In the early days of Dorling Kindersley our knowledge of how to penetrate it was pretty limited. A reconnaissance of the acres occupied by the German publishing community in the halls of Frankfurt would give you an idea of who the leading players were, but very little insight into the size and scope of the remainder. Peter Kindersley decided that the only way to find out was to visit them in their own territory. I drew up a list of likely candidates for illustrated reference books and we flew to the Swiss border where we hired a car and set off into the hinterland: Ravensburg – Munich – Stuttgart – Frankfurt – Cologne – Hamburg – and sundry diversions in between.

We knew not what to expect. Sometimes a company occupied an impressive multi-storey block, sometimes a large suburban villa, and on one occasion in a remote rural location, the smoke-filled front room of a modest cottage. In spite of a number of dead ends, it was a worthwhile experience, and we returned with a portfolio of about 50 publishers with whom there might be mutual interest. The principal learning factor on that trip, though, was the extraordinary power of the book clubs, of which the Bertelsmann group had three major strands, while the Holtzbrink group had the single biggest player. If you were in the habit of dealing with Bertelsmann you were unlikely to get any of your lead titles selected by Holtzbrink, and vice versa.

Over the years we did a lot of business with the Bertelsmann clubs, and with the EBG especially whose commissioning publisher, Dr Dietrich Schaefer, became a key customer and a firm friend. It was he who selected *The Amateur Naturalist* as a main selection and commissioned *The Garden Book* as another. An order for 200,000 copies was a brilliant starting point for a project, with the rest of the world to play for. Dietrich Schaefer was also indirectly responsible for the book that, above all others, was to play a critical role in the future direction of the company. Before he left EBG to become the founding head of SDK, the German rights office we established in his home town of Stuttgart, he told me that the book club was looking for a new version of a trusted perennial for an upcoming main selection – *How Things Work*.

It was a relatively easy option for DK to pick up, but it was hard to think of a novel way of approaching the subject other than the conventional two-colour diagrams of the insides of machines, with a lot of arrows indicating process. The solution was fortuitous and serendipitous. Linda, my wife, was then the children's publisher at Collins, and one of the first books she acquired there in the early 1970s had been *Cathedral* by David Macaulay. She had subsequently published all his architectural titles, had been a witness to his marriage, and as a result David had become a close family friend. Married publishers don't usually nick one another's authors – not at least without major repercussions – but one evening, when David was staying with us and we were enjoying a pre-dinner drink (Linda was in the kitchen), I was suddenly struck by the revelation that the solution to our constipated thinking about the German book club commission was sipping a gin and tonic across the room from me. Opportunism overcame my conjugal scruples; in fact, it overwhelmed them. I asked him if he would like the challenge of a really big idea, a new and radical approach to the story of how everything works.

'Sure. Why not?' he said. 'Sounds great.'

So it began. The first spreads made ready for Frankfurt 1985 were intriguing but mystifying, especially to our own rights team. But the following year, when we had hammered out the concept and David was able to work with the disciplined London support of Alan Buckingham, Neil Ardley, David Burnie and Peter Luff, it was clear that this was going to develop into a uniquely engaging work. During the three years that it took to complete, David flew back and forth from Rhode Island, stayed in our house and drew at an oval table in our sitting room after his days in the office. The impossible-to-ignore presence near his feet of Sam, our generously inflated black lab, may have had something to do with David's creation of a large woolly mammoth – the character that brought warmth and humour to the book.

For DK, *The Way Things Work* was an accidental bestseller. Rather than being a book conceived and originated by an in-house team working with an author, as pretty much every other DK book was, this was the product of an author/illustrator's genius supported by the design and editorial rigours of a DK team. But we had no idea it was going to be the runaway bestseller it became. Nor did Houghton Mifflin, David's US publisher. As the book was so late being completed, there were hardly any proofs available at the ABA of May 1988, and therefore the aisles of the convention centre did not rustle with the expectant whisperings of booksellers who have spotted Christmas coming early to their store. In fact, Christmas did not come at all for some of them. Houghton had ordered a first print run of 100,000 copies, which we delivered in October. They had hardly publicised the book at all (on the "not invented here" principle, despite David being one of their star authors), but it disappeared off the shelves like the proverbial greased lightning. Dads bought it for boys, boys bought it for dads, mums bought it for both of them – the perfect cross-generational gift. But we couldn't meet the demand. There was no way we could ship them a reprint from Europe in time to replenish their stocks in the holiday season. The vanishing of *The Way Things Work* became a cause célèbre. Even *Time* magazine ran a story on it, likening the book to the stealth bomber as no one could find it.

Paradoxically, the delay increased the suspense and the desire. When it came back into print in early 1989, it sold and sold, nearly 600,000 copies that year in trade hardback sales alone. It was our first appearance on the US bestseller charts, a title that had begun with a book club conversation in Stuttgart (ironically, the club never took *TWTW* – it was too unconventional for them), progressed by way of a chance encounter in my own home (my marriage survived), teased the American public with its scarcity, and became a worldwide hit. It would subsequently play a major part in DK's fortunes for years, leading, among other things, to the arrival of Bill Gates at the door of No 9 Henrietta Street.

In 1988, however, we were experiencing our first full year in partnership with Reader's Digest. From the launch of the breakthrough *Eyewitness* series in the spring and the publication of *The Way Things Work* in the autumn, they

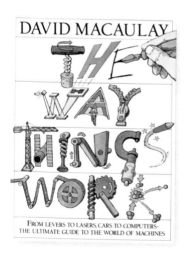

David Macaulay's masterwork is probably the most famous, and for many the best loved, of all DK books. Not only did it sell millions of copies, it was instrumental in Microsoft investing in DK, and subsequently became a top-selling CD-ROM.

might have expected to see a hike in our turnover and profits. But our accounting year ran July-June, the *Eyewitness* books had not had enough time to sell through by mid-summer, and it was too early to take in income from the Macaulay book. The figures for that year, 1978-88, show DK stagnant at £10 million turnover, a misleading snapshot of a company that was in reality poised for a spectacular leap forward. Did the Digest appreciate that? It is hard to say. We were probably too small to register on their radar in any meaningful way. If we were only going to contribute modestly to their coffers, and they had at the same time to deal with the everyday irritant of Peter Kindersley behaving (as they probably saw it) like a demented wombat, they probably concluded that it was barely worth the management time they were obliged to give us.

From our point of view the atmosphere was not helped by the fact that they had turned down *Eyewitness* (too new, too radical?) and *The Way Things Work* (too wacky, too unorthodox?). To us, and Peter in particular, it signalled that they were mired in the dreary conservatism of their meat-and-potatoes readership and unable, or at least unwilling, to exercise any degree of entrepreneurial risk.

The immediate effect of our publishing two such high-profile projects as *Eyewitness* and *The Way Things Work* was that our customer base around the world doubled as we made our mark with children's publishers. There was no question of limiting ourselves to these two successes – those publishers who had acquired *Eyewitness* wanted more of it, and more like it; those who had failed to acquire it wanted another series, different but carved from the same dramatic rock face. A whole vista of juvenile reference publishing opened up before us, from pre-school to teens, a raft of titles and series that all had three things in common – they were photographic, their covers were white, and they were in demand.

Growth, in DK terms, implied that more staff were being hired and more office space was being occupied. Given the labour intensity of every book, each new project could involve taking on up to four extra staff, and whether they were on a part-time or full-time basis they still needed a seat on which to plant their bum and a screen on which to fix their gaze. Similarly, with the escalation of the foreign publisher clientele and the penetration of new publishing territories, the foreign rights team required additional personnel.

DK's international sales record is one of the great publishing success stories – and it still continues today. In the beginning there were just the four of us, trying to scoop up bits of the world without much in the way of linguistic skills. We soon discovered our limitations. If you visit one of the haughtier French publishers in his Parisian lair, he is unlikely to grant you his best attention if your basic communication is in Franglais. As soon as Annie Blanc (later Frankland) joined DK to specialise in her native French market, the sales were dramatically transformed. Antony Melville, a gifted multi-linguist but especially fluent in Italian, made a comparable difference in that country. Mary Holman, Katherine Thompson and Nicky Strong gave a boost to Spanish language sales, both on the mainland and in Latin America. (*Eyewitness*, for example, was sold in five separate co-editions – Castilian, Catalan, Basque,

Gallego and Mexican Spanish.) The establishment of SDK in Stuttgart enabled the expansion of German book deals, and, later, after the fall of the Berlin Wall and the opening up of Eastern Europe, the Insiders agency in Bratislava, run by Peter and Maria Hroziencik, grew a remarkable business from being able to travel and negotiate in multiple languages between Slovenia and Siberia. So it went on. Sales assistants or managers fluent in Japanese, Korean, Chinese, even Thai, joined the team, and another office was established in Portugal as a co-venture with Civilizacao. There was also a formidable array of talents selling over the years to the English language markets, notably Netie Brooke, Simonne Waud, Paget Hetherington, Vicky Dawbarn, Mary Thompson and Jacky Spigel. Jacky also served a long term of duty in the Scandinavian markets before giving way to Rachel Watson.

In 1989, however, the immediate priority was to add a children's rights team to supplement the adult sales force, especially in the larger markets which required a doubling up of personnel to cover the territory. It was as much a physical requirement as a business one; there was no way of avoiding the packhorse duties of carrying multiple art bags stuffed with presentation materials – dummy books, sample spreads on heavy boards, bundles of proofs, sales documents. It was heavy work tramping the streets, piling it all into the back of a taxi, hauling the bags into a reception area and then into lifts and along corridors to a publisher's office. After a few years of these backbreaking duties you could recognise DK sales veterans on the street by the simian length of their arms.

The fact that we now needed a children's sales person for every major market, and that the demand for the expansion of that list showed no sign of abating, led inevitably to the creation of two separate divisions in the company. Mike Strong, who had set up and run DK's own UK sales force, became managing director of the children's division, Sue Unstead was already in place as editorial director, and Ruth Sandys, while still international sales director, moved across to specialise in the children's area. Alan Buckingham headed up the adult division, with various editorial directors – Jackie Douglas, Daphne Razazan, David Lamb – reporting to him, and Michael Devenish, who had joined the company from Harper Collins as deputy to Ruth Sandys, now assumed the role of international sales director for adult books. The children's division moved into newly leased premises in King Street.

Splitting in two, both creatively and commercially, was the right thing to do. It enabled both divisions to concentrate on growing their categories and it gave the sales people a more focused direction. In any event, the overall expansion of the company demanded it. By June 1989, the year-end revenues had grown by £7 million to £17 million. And the staff had almost doubled.

If You Build It, They Will Come

Control, control, control was the Kindersley mantra – over what we created, how it was produced, manufactured, marketed and sold, how it was stored and retained for future use in different formats and on other platforms. (Oddly, in one of those management consultant tests where personalities are assessed, he did not emerge as a control freak – which might say something about the validity of the testing method.) The principle of owning what we originated was a cardinal rule, one that was crucial in building the backbone of the company and, later, in enhancing its net value.

The first major testing of this principle occurred with the determination to produce the most comprehensively illustrated encyclopedia of garden plants of all time. We could see the opportunity – the competition (from Reader's Digest) had been very successful but was beginning to look dated, especially in its design. How to beat it? There was nothing to be gained from acquiring all the photographs from picture agencies. The images probably wouldn't deliver a significant point of difference to the Digest book and, more importantly, we wouldn't be able to exploit them for future spin-offs without paying rights fees all over again. The only solution was to create a photographic database of our own, and to do that thoroughly we would need to take somewhere in the region of 15,000 images. The problem, in the mid '80s, when we began to develop this project, was how to make the numbers work. We could see the mountain, and we could envisage the view from the top if we conquered it, but for now we couldn't afford the equipment to climb it. Year after year we took the dummy presentation spreads to Frankfurt, the prospective buyers gazed at them admiringly and then politely enquired when the finished book would be available, to which there was no convincing answer.

Then two things happened to transform the situation – the opportunism of a literary agent, and a change in fiscal policy.

The attitude of literary agents to Dorling Kindersley was variable. Some erroneously dismissed us as packagers who wouldn't pay royalties and therefore unworthy of courtship. A few took no interest in our kind of books on the snobbish pretext that this wasn't publishing worthy of the name. But there was, fortunately, a group that could see opportunities for their authors, and themselves, in being associated with a company that had developed such a formidable network of publishing partnerships around the world. The royalty rates might be lower than conventional trade houses would pay, but the overall rewards if you took worldwide sales into account, could be comparable. At DK we viewed authors as our partners in creating the books; we were co-authors, in that neither party could produce the work without the other, and our input – from editors, designers, researchers, photographers or illustrators – was at least 50 per cent, and in many instances, much more. The royalty rates therefore reflected this sharing of endeavour.

Foremost among the agents who saw the potential of building a client list with DK was Felicity Bryan. From the earliest days of the company, while she was still at Curtis Brown, she introduced us to a string of authors whose names would feature on our books, starting with Francis Crick, who wrote the foreword to *The Origin of Johnny*, and continuing through Judy Brittain (*The Encyclopedia of Needlecraft*), Mary Gilliatt (*The Decorating Book*), Ralph Denyer (*The Guitar Handbook*), and Gerald Durrell. Subsequently, when she had set up her own agency, she brought us, among others, Miriam Stoppard, John Brookes, Yan-Kit So, Mary Berry, Penelope Hobhouse and Joanna Simon. Felicity was assiduous in finding us authors to fit a particular topic and also in bringing us names who might take us into new areas. It was a symbiotic relationship from which both parties benefited, and it is to her credit that when the half-yearly royalty statements were despatched, the biggest cheque of all was consistently made out to her agency.

While we were struggling to get the garden plants encyclopedia off the ground we had made it clear to anyone who cared to listen that, aside from it being illustrated throughout with entirely new photography, what it really needed to give it both authenticity and commercial clout was the endorsement of the Royal Horticultural Society. We had managed to scale the walls of the First Aid societies, of the American and British Medical Associations, of Good Housekeeping, Reader's Digest, the British Museum and the Natural History Museum, but we could find no way of breaching the ramparts of the RHS. Felicity came to our rescue. In a moment of serendipity she found herself seated at dinner one night next to the ultimate supremo of that organisation and by the end of the evening her charms had persuaded him that the RHS could benefit from being represented by a literary agent. Thus, thanks to her, we struck a deal for the endorsement of the title and at the same time acquired the priceless horticultural expertise of the Director General of the RHS, Christopher Brickell, as editor-in-chief.

In spite of this tremendous boost, it was still impossible to make the book's profit and loss statement work. It was going to be a loss leader for years. Then, one day, with one neat lateral sidestep, the accounts department came up with a solution: capitalise the photographic database. The DK Picture Library was born, and thereafter every image produced and owned by the company was archived within it. It quickly required full-time management. In parallel with the plant pictures pouring in from gardens all over the UK, a flood of images was filling the library from the expanding adult and children's lists which had by now adopted the all-pervasive style of cut-out photographs on white backgrounds, most of these shot in the DK Photo Studio.

The launch of *The RHS Gardeners' Encyclopedia of Plants & Flowers* in the autumn of 1989 was a sensation. It was a testament to the belief we had about certain major reference titles, best summed up by the line in the movie, *Field of Dreams*: 'If you build it, they will come'. Everybody wanted it – the trade, the book clubs, and the RHS itself for sale to its large membership. At 600 pages it was difficult enough for the production department to keep the reprints on track with the demand. But the momentum was stalled just as the Christmas rush was peaking by the near-total dysfunction of AA Distributors, who were warehousing and delivering our list.

Warehousing and distribution are at the bottom of the publishing food chain. In good times publishers may spend surplus cash upgrading their systems; in bad times these are the first to face neglect. It is ironic that, as publishing itself evolved from the cheerful, sometimes desperate, amateurism of the post-war years to become a slicker, more professional business, the industry continued to be bedevilled by serial mismanagements at the distribution end. If I have one recurring nightmare about my three decades at DK, it features the malfunctioning of a warehouse. Unsurprisingly. It happened five times – with the AA in 1989; with Tiptree, owned by Random House, in 1993/4 (when we were a plc and sales downturns were ill-received by the city); with IBD, owned, ironically, by Pearson, in 1999 (the year before they acquired DK); with our own distribution system in the US a year or so later, after the new warehouse commissioned by the last managing director on the back of his experience in the music industry proved to be unsuited to the delivery of books; and, most recently, with Pearson's own disastrous move from

Harmondsworth to Rugby. On every occasion, apart from the first, we had to publicly explain the fall-off in sales resulting from these third-party fiascos. Frustratingly, whatever one said in justification of the downturn, it was always received with a degree of scepticism as if we were conveniently using the excuse of systemic failure to cover a weakness in the publishing programme.

In the run-up to Christmas 1989 we were answerable to no one except our partners at the Digest. We were simply angry enough and bull-headed enough to take the matter into our own hands and ensure that a book that we had spent five years developing and had "bestseller" written all over it, would reach the public who wanted it. Thus, for several Saturdays, the

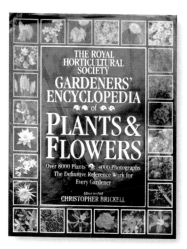

The first, and biggest selling, of the range of gardening reference works DK has produced in association with the RHS. The many thousands of photographs of garden plants specially taken for this title formed the basis of DK's Picture Library that ultimately held more than 2 million images.

directors and senior management could be found with their sleeves rolled up in the AA warehouse, physically lifting the books off the despatch line and packing them into cartons.

The RHS Gardeners' Encyclopedia of Plants & Flowers did achieve bestseller status; over the years it racked up seven-figure sales in the UK alone, along with multiple editions overseas, and it continues as a backlist staple that benefits from regular updating and revising. The relationship with the RHS was not always smooth – it depended on the priorities of changing regimes at the top of that organisation – but it was highly productive. One huge reference tome followed another – *The RHS Encyclopedia of Gardening, RHS A-Z Encyclopedia of Garden Plants* – and then numerous other volumes at differing formats and price points which sprang from the original vision of creating a library of garden plant photography.

The DK gardening list grew into a very potent category and raised our profile significantly. But it is a subject that generally relies heavily on UK and North European sales. It was a given within the company that we would always think globally. Over the years editors and designers were ingrained with the notion that the verbal and visual content of a book should not feel alien to a reader whether they were opening it in Turin, Tokyo, Tulsa, Tübingen or Tunbridge Wells. The white backgrounds helped enormously in this respect; they removed any connotations of nationalist bias or class. But we also had to be alert to the costs of adaptation in those markets where some changes were essential if the book was to work on a practical level. Gardening books were particularly sensitive to differences in climate and seasonality. If you specified that a flower should be planted in January, this translated into high summer in Australia (where north-facing gardens are also sunnier than south-facing), and to a range of possibilities in the climate zones of the US, which made it essential to include a map of the last predicted frosts all the way from Maine to Arizona. In the case of *The RHS Gardeners' Encyclopedia of Plants & Flowers*, this was seen as such a compelling property that the Reader's Digest branch in Australia acquired the rights and spent a huge sum changing the plant catalogue to suit their market. With great success. In the US we sold the rights to Macmillan who, regrettably, published the title with only minimal adaptation. It still sold quite impressively – to those in that market with a love of English gardening – but we did not make the same mistake with the subsequent volumes which we adapted in conjunction with the American Horticultural Society and published ourselves as fully bona fide editions for a US readership. This was expensive to do but there was never any doubt in our minds that this was the right approach to creating a durable backlist.

The fact that *The RHS Gardeners' Encyclopedia of Plants & Flowers* had displaced the RD UK volume as the pre-eminent title on the subject was hardly conducive to a thaw in our relationship with that office. Their American headquarters, however, must have noticed the effect on the figures. By the end of the financial year in June 1990, the combined effect of that book plus *Eyewitness*, *The Way Things Work*, and a raft of other strong supporting titles, was to grow DK's revenues to £26 million, an increase of more than 50 per cent.

Over and Out

America. Our new found land. The starting point for almost every global Dorling Kindersley book. Without the significant print run and the upfront commitment from a US publisher to a title it was usually impossible to make the numbers work. Thus New York was the first port of call with our portfolio of new ideas. Several times a year, laden like mules with our cargo of art bags, we tramped the steaming sidewalks and rode the elevators skywards to sweeten the imagination of this or that publisher with our catalogue of promises. Over the years we became familiars on their beat, and they in turn became our friends and advocates, and taught us much about their business.

By the summer of 1990, having bolstered our reputation in the US from the delivery of the mega-selling *Eyewitness* series and *The Way Things Work*, our confidence was high. It seemed that there was an infinite number of projects we could develop with the new immediacy of our design. With seemingly little risk attached to the sales, why, apart from the funding cash flow, would we license our future list to a publisher rather than assume the role ourselves? We could see the measurable degree by which Knopf's revenues for *Eyewitness* and Houghton Mifflin's for *The Way Things Work* far outstripped our share, and yet we had been responsible for the conception and delivery of those titles. Those houses would not – could not – have created them. They had bought them in, and their only responsibility was to market and sell them. An easy win.

That, of course, is a simplification, but it fuelled our thinking that we could make the transition from packager to publisher and plant DK as an imprint on those shores. History did not favour us – it positively frowned upon the idea. The US was littered with the bones of British publishing houses that had attempted the giant leap across the water; Collins, under the Collins World imprint, had become the latest to abandon the struggle. Peter Kindersley, predictably, had no time for such received wisdom, just as he had no patience in general with the conventions of traditional UK publishers whom he broadly classified as dozy relics of a prehistoric era. He demanded that Richard Harman run the numbers, and then run them again and again, to prove to us that publishing our own list in the US would be a sound proposition. Those who mentioned the potential pitfalls in such a venture were quickly dismissed as lily-livered non-combatants. Like the invasion of Normandy, the issue soon assumed the certainty of a foregone conclusion. The question was when and how.

By the time of the ABA in May 1990 we had decided that

we would restrict the number of titles on display to those that, for whatever reason, we would sell on to a third party publisher. At the same convention we launched the search for the right person to head up the US operation, at first by discreet word of mouth and later via a head-hunter. The convention was in Las Vegas, where the outside temperature hovered around 112 degrees, hot enough to bake your brains and banish reason. But in that crazy heat, and in that crazy setting, it didn't seem inappropriate that we were enjoying the biggest gamble of our business lives to date.

In September the selection process had settled on Steven Sussmann, recently of Avon, a smart, fast-talking, uninhibited guy with no shortage of confidence in his own abilities. Importantly, he was bounding with energy to get stuck into the job and put DK on the publishing map. As he tells it, the only opposition he faced was from his own parents, who doubted whether a bunch of English goyim would be trustworthy employers.

Beth Chang, our very first US employee, had helped find and set up premises on two floors at 232 Madison Avenue. Gradually we staffed up: Allison Devlin joined as publicity manager, Penelope Chaplin as rights manager, while Beth Chang handled promotions. We also persuaded Pam Thomas, a long-term friend and fan of DK, who had acquired titles from us for Crown, to come in as VP associate publisher. The remaining staff, among them Jeanette Mall, Chuck Wills and Ray Rogers, formed the editorial team responsible for the Americanisation or adaptation of the imported DK titles.

The earliest possible launch date was the fall of 1991.

Given that the majority of our forthcoming list had been licensed well before the decision to start publishing, there was only a limited number of titles to fill our inaugural catalogue – 26 in fact. It was a bit threadbare, it included a handful of make-weights that we hadn't been able to license, but at the heart of the collection were some gems that we had saved for this moment and which would serve us well, among them *The Ultimate Horse Book*, *My First Word Book*, and the *Visual Dictionaries*.

These somewhat meagre offerings were insufficient for us to set up our own sales and distribution, but DK's reputation and potential were enough to attract the interest of a range of publishers keen to bolster their own sales operations. Steven Sussmann organised a beauty parade for us to meet – Random House, Putnam, Workman, Simon and Schuster, and Houghton Mifflin. We had expected Random House to be the front runner as 50 per cent of our backlist was with one or other of their imprints, their reps were familiar with DK books, and their reputation as the best sales force in the land was well acknowledged. There was the additional factor that our overall level of returns within the RH group was impressively low, somewhere around ten per cent. But when we met Bruce Harris and Gerry Harrison to discuss the way forward, they appeared somewhat restrained in their enthusiasm. And when we enquired about how much time we would be given at their sales conference to present the DK list, the answer was 'approximately one hour'. The idea of flying to Florida or Puerto Rico in December for a three-day binge was very appealing, but the prospect of being such a marginal vessel in the group's huge fleet of imprints was a major downer.

Phyllis Grann, who had recently taken a cleaver to Putnam's baggy list and slashed its annual output to 70 titles, offered a brief, somewhat chilly, presentation and subsequently bowed out of the running. The Workman option was attractive in that, although we had never sold them a title, we had long admired Peter Workman's quirky, eclectic, hands-on style of publishing and its commercially targeted directness. But his sales force was almost entirely made up of commissioned reps, which made us wonder if we could harness collective in-house support. Charlie Hayward at Simon and Schuster led an impressively spirited advocacy of his company's strengths. We had history with S&S, which dated back to the early days when Knopf/Random House adopted our first titles. There was bad blood between those two companies from the time when Bob Gottlieb and Tony Schulte left S&S to join their big rivals, and Dick Snyder played on it with us by forging a close relationship with Mitchell Beazley. For years we were greeted inside the S&S building with ill-concealed hauteur and never succeeded in selling them a book. In recent years, however, a new regime and the charismatic presence of Caroline Herter in their illustrated books division meant that a healthy publishing relationship was formed between us. It was therefore tempting to sign up with S&S. The fact that we ultimately chose Houghton Mifflin was dependent on the relatively modest size of their list. DK would not be a tiny imprint among many, the sales and marketing people had the capacity to give us as much attention as we needed, and, most telling of all, we could have a whole day at their sales conference to promote our list. HM might have appeared a less overtly commercial publisher than the other contenders, but the relative visibility of our books in their reps' bags was one deciding factor. The other was our liking of, and trust in, Joe Kanon, the HM publisher. Over the succeeding years that faith was borne out – he gave his word and he kept it, and we have much to thank him for.

The move toward publishing in the US became a bone of contention with Reader's Digest. To them it was headstrong and ill-considered; it went against the grain of their risk-free business ethos. The words 'goose' and 'golden egg' cropped up frequently. The more they demurred, the more determined Peter Kindersley became to push it through. The relationship, never harmonious, deteriorated into general acrimony until, one day, we, the senior directors – Peter, Richard, myself – were ordered to attend a summit meeting with George Grune, CEO of RD, in Pleasantville at ten o'clock on a Monday morning. We arranged to fly to New York on the Sunday, but when we arrived at Heathrow it was blanketed in fog, which hung around all day and forced the cancellation of most outgoing flights. The only way we could get to Pleasantville in time for the meeting was to take the Monday morning Concorde flight.

'Can we afford this?' asked Peter.

'Yes, of course we can,' said Richard. 'Anyway, we don't have a choice.'

It was company policy that everyone flew economy class, unless the flight was fifteen hours or longer. With such a large international sales force constantly in the air, it would have been impossible to bear the annual expense of business class tickets, and, at the same time, it was part of the collegiate company spirit that there should be no culture of "us and them". In the office everyone was on first name terms with everyone else; the in-house phone directory was in Christian name order; the directors' doors were always open to anyone who wanted to drop in and ask a question, show a layout, request a signature, and so forth. So if ever one of us was lucky enough to earn an upgrade on a flight, it felt like a win on the lottery. And to travel on Concorde – that was game, set and match.

We touched down at JFK in buoyant mood, pleasantly fortified from our champagne brunch, and slid into the limo waiting to drive us north to Pleasantville. As soon as we walked into George Grune's office, however, we realised that this was to be no cosy get-together. It felt like the Cuban missile crisis. George Grune was a powerfully built ex-marine with close-cropped hair. The sleeves of his crisp white shirt were rolled back to reveal a Rolex bulging on his massive wrist like a hand grenade. Everything in his manner indicated that he was ready to pull the pin and spatter these upstart limeys across the Impressionists on his wall.

'I'm getting a lot of unwelcome feedback from my colleagues here,' he growled. 'They don't like the way you talk to them, and I don't like the way you talk about them. I've had enough frankly. I don't think this partnership is working.'

'I agree,' said Peter unhesitatingly. 'What do you suggest we do about it?'

'I don't believe you are bringing significant financial benefits, and, as you know, we are sceptical about your move to publish in this market. I suggest we agree a fair valuation and you find the means to buy yourselves out of the relationship.'

That was the end of the meeting. It had been brusque, brief and business-like. A long way to come to be carpeted for fifteen minutes, but it felt like a victory, not a humiliation. As we drove through the gates we punched the air, and immediately began planning the next move. How much would RD want? Would we be able to borrow it, or would we need another strategic partner? If so, who were the candidates and could they find compatibility with Peter Kindersley where RD had found only irreconcilable differences? How much would our independence of spirit – such a vital ingredient in the growth of the company, one that the Digest had threatened to stifle – be compromised by a new liaison? There was much to ponder...

That night we flew back to London, economy class, in the back of a packed 747. We didn't care. We were in celebratory mood. Two highs in one crowded morning – the flight on Concorde, and the freedom pass from Reader's Digest. The costs of those air tickets shrivelled into insignificance. It was a defining day.

Thanks, Bill

There were three principal players in the frame to become Dorling Kindersley's next partner – Larousse, Mondadori and Bonnier. All three were viable candidates in that they were long-established customers of our books and each could have brought substantial benefits to our business. Ebbe Carlson at Bonnier was probably the most determined – he was certainly the most persistent. While Peter was mulling over the options, a curious sequence of events intervened.

Microsoft in 1990 was scouring the world in its search for intellectual properties to acquire – galleries, photo archives, publishing assets. One day, one of Bill Gates's missionaries, Ed Kelly, came by the office to enquire about the digital rights to *The Way Things Work*. He met with John Adams who was in the process of setting up DK Vision to exploit our content in video and broadcast programming. *The Way Things Work* was top of John's list. In the course of the conversation John realised that Microsoft might be interested in acquiring more of DK than just the rights to a single title, so he directed Ed Kelly towards Peter Kindersley's office.

There was no doubt that this was a very interesting, if completely unexpected, development. Immediately Peter saw the advantages of tying up with the pioneer of the new technology over being harnessed to the old wagons of the publishing world, however venerable they might be. At the same time we could all see that we would be linking up with a culture very different from our own. Yet again.

Negotiations took place in London and Seattle. There seemed to be goodwill on both sides to make something happen, though it was inevitably laced with a fair dose of paranoia. On his next trip to the UK, Ed Kelly, a slim, quiet, relatively ascetic character, was accompanied by the contrasting figure of Min Yee, another senior Microsoft player made seriously wealthy from their generous stock options scheme (the number plate on his latest fast car read THANKS BILL). Min Yee was a force of nature. Part Chinese, part Native American, he was heavily built but appeared even bulkier when he marched through Covent Garden's chilly streets in his huge coyote overcoat with his long black hair falling down to his shoulders. You could hear him a mile away as he spouted off about everything under the sun, spraying from topic to topic like a garden hose but never dwelling on one long enough to threaten his boredom threshold, which was about ten seconds max. He was like a creature from an animated cartoon, and his gargantuan appetites matched his personality, as he demonstrated at the DK Christmas party. A month later, when the negotiations were well underway, I invited him to my home to watch the Super Bowl. Not knowing his dietary preferences, Linda had thoughtfully cooked two main dishes, one meat, the other vegetarian. Min was not particular – he had two large helpings of each. When we went upstairs to the sitting room to watch the game, he seemed surprisingly uninterested in the football but lay flat out on the carpet like a beached whale, burping and eructating with such vigour I could hardly hear the commentary. It was a shame that not long after the deal with Microsoft was done that spring, he departed the company. He was a breath of (not always) fresh air and we missed the Falstaffian entertainment he provided.

In addition to DK setting up Vision as a separate business, Peter was also keen to establish Multimedia. And, naturally, *The Way Things Work* was the prize project slated to be developed as a CD-ROM. This, of course, was what Microsoft had originally come shopping for. It therefore became a tricky element in the negotiations between the two companies as to where that would reside, and who would create the electronic version. Ultimately this was a battle DK won, but in exchange we were obliged to create other material that would become part of Microsoft's database for its Encarta project.

In February 1991 the deal to buy back the 50 per cent stake from Reader's Digest was concluded at a remarkably modest price. A month later, for a substantially higher sum, Bill Gates acquired a 26 per cent holding. It gave us a platform for growth and was heralded in the press as a visionary leap forward into a future that nobody yet understood but everyone recognised as likely to be meaningful and transformative. The announcement also focused on the virtues of building up databases of content. Certainly, when the Microsoft lawyers had crawled all over our offices in the preceding months, the principal target of their interest was the availability of, and access to, the digital rights in every DK book. The long-held principle of owning what we produced proved its worth in spades on this occasion and undoubtedly boosted the value of the company in Microsoft's eyes.

The internal euphoria at the deal, which didn't interfere with our independence and which took us forward to a new platform of content development, was abruptly snuffed out. Bill Gates, as we came to understand, doesn't like part-ownership of enterprises. What he wants, he wants to own and he wants to control. No sooner had the ink dried on the contracts between DK and Microsoft than their true colours were revealed. Heavyweight accountants and apparatchiks prowled through the warren of buildings in Henrietta Street, chucking out caustic asides like rampaging movie moguls.

'You guys have got no back-up systems.'

'Your accounts are a shambles.'

'What a bunch of amateurs.'

'This company is going bust.'

It was extraordinary behaviour, designed to bully and intimidate. Leading the affray was Frank Gaudette, Microsoft CFO, who was joining the DK board as their representative. At the first meeting he sat down at the table while his financial sidekicks set up a flipchart.

'Now then, gentlemen,' said Frank, 'we have decided that this company's prospects are not overly auspicious and we would like to make you an offer to acquire 100 per cent of the business.'

Before anyone could respond, the number cruncher at the flipchart started posting up figures.

'This is where DK is today, this is where it will be next year, in three years, in five years…' He then put up another figure. 'We have made a calculation and, as you can see, we are prepared to offer you far more than its worth today in exchange for complete ownership.'

Silence. As board members, we all had shares and share options. They were aiming right at our wallets. It was more money than most, if not all, of us had dreamed of.

'Frank,' said Peter Kindersley after a long pause. 'There is another scenario.'

'What's that?'

'We make plans to float the company.'

This may have been in the back of Peter's mind for a while, and he may have been encouraged to think about it by Richard, who had had experience of taking a company to market. But it hadn't yet been widely discussed as a definite target in our ambitions.

'Very well,' said Frank, 'we will take two votes. Firstly, hands up those in favour of the Microsoft acquisition.'

None of us moved. Only Frank raised his hand.

'Second, hands up those in favour of public flotation.'

We all raised our hands. Except Frank.

But as soon as the vote was taken, Frank's demeanour changed utterly. The accountants folded away the flipcharts and disappeared. Frank shook Peter by the hand.

'That's absolutely great!' he said. 'It will be fantastic to bring this company to market and you can count on me to give you all the backing you need. I know something about it as I've done it many times before.'

This was an astonishing turnaround. The brief window into the dark side of Microsoft's corporate culture had been chilling, but we realised that we were going to have to swim with the big barracudas now and there was no point being precious about such behaviour. As for Frank Gaudette, he became a wonderful supporter of DK in every way, visited our stand at book fairs and was as friendly and generous as one could have wished. It was a great sadness to all of us that he contracted cancer and died before fulfilling his aim of taking us public.

One of the reasons Microsoft might have thought DK was vulnerable to takeover was the rate at which we were expanding and the effect that was having on our cash flow. 1991 proved to be a year of feverish growth on a multitude of fronts, laudable in its ambitions but challenging to a stretched management. DK Vision was set up, under John Adams and the newly recruited Simon Jollands, an individual of such bouncy optimism he made Tigger look like a depressive. DK Multimedia was founded under Alan Buckingham, who initially needed persuading to leave his current role as MD of Adult Books but who was the only viable choice for the job in that he combined extensive experience of producing books according to DK values with a higher degree of computer literacy than anyone else on the creative side. DK Education was formed to sell packs into schools under the direction of Mike Strong, who left Children's to be replaced by Linda

Davis, herself a recent refugee from the mass culling of 60 senior people at Harper Collins. Andrew Heritage also joined from the Times Books division at Harper Collins to set up DK Cartography as a new division and to create our own mapping database. We were also set to launch our first publishing list in the US that fall with all the cash implications connected with that.

In addition to the Adult and Children's divisions, there was another strand of book creation called DK Direct, which had been set up to produce continuity series for the big direct mail companies such as Time-Life, Reader's Digest, Disney and World Book. It had been formed two years previously under the management of Rod Hare, an Australian accountant who had first come to DK in that habitual Aussie way of freelancing in companies, working hard during the week and playing hard at the weekend. Unlike many of his compatriots, who climbed into their VW camper vans and moved on, Rod stayed put – he became part of the furniture, and proved himself such a capable operator that he took up a permanent role and was rewarded with the MD seat at DK Direct. This division was now producing several series, occupied yet another building in Covent Garden, and was rapidly growing its staff numbers. Likewise, the demands for DK Children's books were insatiable, and advertisements for new staff seemed to be a permanent feature in the trade press. In another mini-expansion, Linda's brief was to add to the non-fiction stable a new genre of fiction titles, cast in the DK mould to give a more rounded quality to the list.

Thus we had in that high summer seven creative divisions,

two publishing operations, a turnover of £42 million, a staff of some 400, and no personnel director. We had a new partner and the beginnings of a plan to grow the company to the point where we could take it public, maybe the following year. It sounds crazy but at the time such was the spirit in the place and so great the belief in our products that it felt like surfing. The big wave was coming but we had no fear of riding it.

It was a year of extraordinary contrasts. In the early spring, while Peter and Richard were shuttling back and forth to Seattle to negotiate with Gates, I flew east to accompany Hilary Downie, one of our ever-expanding cast of international sales managers, to explore the possibilities of selling DK books in translation into the Southeast Asian markets. Each year we were notching up new languages on our sales belt, particularly with the *Eyewitness* books, and were now seeking a breakthrough into the teeming millions of Thailand, Indonesia and Malaysia. The journey was made more difficult by the flyover restrictions imposed by the First Gulf War.

With the establishment of these new media divisions, the DK design style was becoming all-pervasive and approaching the status of a brand.

There is no substitute for visiting publishers on their own patch – you learn so much more about them than from a brief encounter at a book fair where a business card may be all they have to prove their existence. There were numerous meetings in Jakarta, Singapore and Kuala Lumpur that afforded some optimism for a way forward, but, as on many other sales trips, there was one episode that one recalls for its bizarre sense of unreality, for the inescapable feeling of "what the hell am I doing here?" It had happened to me in New Zealand when I had arranged to meet the Greenpeace people, with whom we were producing two books, on their boat in Auckland Harbour, and they failed to show up. It happened in Japan when a publisher invited me to experience the traditional tea ceremony in all its discomfiting ritual. When this was over he led me out by a back door accompanied by two geishas, now transformed from chalk-faced shop front dummies into giggling good-time girls, clack-clacking along the pavement in their wooden shoes. We entered a karaoke bar where we sat down at a table, ordered the customary bottle of Ballantine's, stripped off our jackets, rolled back our sleeves, and took it in turns to murder "The House of the Rising Sun". It happened in Mexico City when a two-hour taxi ride in one of those Beetle taxis through the never-ending jam of the metropolis ended with a publisher saying no to every single item in our bags.

Now, here in Bangkok, another long journey approached the surreal. We had been informed that the leading Thai medical publisher was based not in the centre but in the outlying reaches of the city. We grabbed a tuk-tuk. After an hour of crazily dodging the capital's relentless traffic, we reached a remote semi-urban landscape criss-crossed by canals where the muddy terrain was crowded with hut-like dwellings. Washing hung on lines, pigs and ducks and chickens wandered in and around the houses, piles of rubbish smouldered in the sullen, steamy air and a smell of rancour and neglect pervaded the atmosphere. Images of war were occupying my mind – between here and home a conflict was being fought of which we knew few details apart from the headlines on CNN. Now, as our tuk-tuk battled through the potholes and threw us around in its unforgiving interior, it felt uncannily similar to *Apocalypse Now*. Even though we were on a mission, not to find Kurtz, but a publisher of medical books, it still felt like a journey into the heart of darkness. Finally we arrived at a brick two-storey house. There was no indication that this was a business address. Chickens pecked in the yard, an old woman was sweeping the step. After some misunderstandings in sign language, she let us in and took us to the first floor where a neatly dressed man was seated at a table. A few books were stacked on one shelf of a bookcase.

'You are a medical publisher, yes?' asked Hilary brightly.

'Yes. Medical books.'

'I wrote to you about our medical encyclopedia. Did you receive that?'

'Yes.'

'So, what do you think? Are you interested in buying the rights?'

'No. Sorry. Too big.'

End of meeting.

By contrast, three months later we were in New York City,

launching the inaugural DK Inc list to booksellers at the ABA with as much fizz and fanfare as we could muster. This huge early summer bun fight was the one fixed point on the American calendar, when publishers, publicists, reps, retailers, authors, agents, printers, distributors and wannabees assembled from all corners of the republic to ramp their offerings for the fall season. In complete contrast to the dour austerity of the Frankfurt halls, this was a combination of a circus and a playpen in which participants spared no expense in devising cheesy ways of attracting attention. Publishers competed to offer the most sought-after giveaways – tote bags, T-shirts, badges, balloons, candy, cookies and key rings – while authors signed advance copies of their books, and booksellers waddled the aisles with trolleys laden with accumulated freebies.

DK had spared no expense on their booth nor on the logo-emblazoned tote bags, which proved so popular that lines formed round the block and normally mild-mannered librarians came to blows when the stocks were running low. Stuart Jackman had brought his trademark clean-cut design touch to the decoration of the stand, the promotional and publicity details, the catalogue, and the book covers. The DK look was everywhere. The response was terrific. It felt like a new beginning.

Home Deliveries

Michael Devenish was (still is) a gentleman farmer. He wore a blazer, cravat and corduroys, had a well-trained gun dog who sat obediently at his feet when visiting the office, and brought baskets of his orchard apples to sustain us at the Frankfurt Book Fair. He was liked by everyone who dealt with him for his warm civility and he was also an MBA. On his daily commute to Dorling Kindersley, where he was international sales director for Adult Books, Michael fell in with a couple of entrepreneurs (one a businessman, the other a doctor) who pitched a direct-selling plan at him that they believed was ideally suited to DK books. After some weeks of being subjected to this, Michael's business brain began to be persuaded that there was indeed some merit in the scheme. He relayed his thoughts to the board, and invited his travelling companions to meet us.

Direct selling into the home was not something we had previously considered. It had acquired a dodgy reputation in the '60s with the collapse of some foot-in-the-door pyramid-selling schemes, and not much had happened since to revive the concept in the publishing world. We knew, however, that Usborne, one of our competitors in the children's book market, was operating a successful home-selling business and that furthermore this was accounting for around 40 per cent of their revenues. Always on the lookout for new sales channels to expand the business beyond the limitations of the traditional book trade, Peter Kindersley was persuaded to give this venture a shot. As there was no built-in expertise anywhere in the company of running this kind of business, we had to buy it in.

The world of direct selling is something else. Certainly something else from the planet we inhabited. The management types who were hired to set up and run DK Family Library (as it was initially called) were unacquainted with book publishing – they had, in former lives, variously learned their trade as purveyors of home crafts, romantic lighting, health supplements, keepsakes, plastic sandwich containers, and adventurous lingerie.

'Basically, we are pedlars of dreams,' said Peter Cartwright, the ever-cheery semi-professional gambler who was appointed managing director. He was a graduate of the naughty knickers group.

'The dream I was selling was, I suppose, romance with an edge,' he added, a trifle lasciviously.

'We have to find dreams to go with our books,' said PK.

'Mr Kindersley, I believe that I am the man who can help you do that.'

Cartwright appealed to Kindersley. He had the chirpiness born of years of salesmanship. He was one of those guys who, come rain or shine, would stand on your doorstep with a smile and a ready quip. But he also knew how to play the big crowds at conferences and have them eat from his hands, especially the women who would always constitute the majority in this type of business.

It quickly transpired that the core of the home-selling operation would be in children's books, partly for reasons of price, partly because they provided a perfect bridge between the school and the home. The timing, as far as DK was concerned, was on the button. Our children's list, with its distinctive images on white backgrounds, was now the most instantly recognisable feature in the non-fiction section of a bookshop. It provided attractive, accessible learning tools at every age level. It is no exaggeration to say that parents and children loved those books, and were hungry for more. Nor was this just a middle class phenomenon. The most interesting thing, to me, about DK Family Library was the range of people it attracted, from bored upper-class wives anxious for some meaningful occupation in their lives to blue-collar mothers who had grown up in homes where there were no books and who were now determined that their own kids be not similarly disadvantaged. They, in particular, became the most fervent advocates, and to see their faces light up when presented with forthcoming titles was among the most rewarding experiences a publisher could have. This seemed like a business that had overtly charitable benefits, and if those people could translate their passion into real sales and thereby generate valuable income for their household, then it was truly a win-win situation for everybody.

The devil, as ever, was in the detail. As nobody in the DK management hierarchy was versed in direct-selling, the whole thing was one long learning curve. The expertise may have been bought in from outside, but the problem was that none of them could agree on the best way forward. They came from different organisations that had operated from different priorities. The idea was to build leaders in the business. The leaders would become leaders by selling more books, and recruiting more distributors. They would take a percentage of the earnings acquired by the distributors they had recruited. Those distributors would likewise recruit more beneath them. Thus pyramids, or family trees, of networking participants would grow multiple branches and become, if all went to plan, substantial generators of income, both for DKFL and for themselves. (The word "pyramid" was never used – in the bad old days of direct selling, there was always a loser in a pyramid scheme. In the DK structure nobody lost.)

The discount scheme was, from the beginning, a problematic issue and had to be revised after a few months when it was proving a disincentive to recruitment. But it was always unclear whether this subdivision of DK's business was going in the right direction. The regular management meetings or board meetings were among the most tedious I ever attended. The DKFL executives all suffered from logorrhoea – I guess it came with the territory – and each was equally convinced of his or her own rightness. One would argue that the emphasis for the next quarter should be on sales; another would proselytise the case for recruitment; a third would demand a rethink on the business model; and a fourth would maintain the signing-on fee was prohibitive. Who could judge which was the most efficacious course to follow? Certainly not Peter Kindersley, who made it up as he went along and, as often as not, changed his mind at the next meeting. It seemed to depend on which of the DKFL team whispered the loudest in his ear.

The most contentious issue, as far as the DKFL distributors were concerned, was the exclusivity of what they were selling. It seems that all successful direct selling businesses have based their pitch on the uniqueness of their offering and its unavailability in any sales channel other than their own. If this was impossible to realise, then the next option would be to market the product at a substantial discount to the high street. At DK there was of course no ready-made list of titles that we could withdraw from other sales outlets and hand over to the first sprinkling of new distributors signing up round the fringes of the M25. They had to act more like a book club and sell on the trade list at a reduced price, which, when you take into account all the costs associated with setting up and running the DKFL operation, plus the percentage of receipts that the distributors would take, severely tested the profit margins on every title. Once again, the endless cycle of boardroom arguments began. If they couldn't have a wholly exclusive list, the DKFL executives argued, then at the very least they needed a certain number of exclusive titles on which to base their marketing and recruitment campaigns and to feature prominently in their quarterly promotion catalogues.

DK itself could not justify the origination costs of the exclusive titles when the sales projections were so minimal. Something had to give. In the end we bit the bullet and began to carve out a range of exclusive loss-leading titles, many of which, it is fair to say, subsequently justified the investment.

The prolonged lack of consensus on discounts, reward schemes, exclusivity, and royalty rates to authors (another thorny issue) contributed to a slower than anticipated start to the business. There was also pressure of a different kind beginning to build in the high street. We could rely on the discounts that DKFL distributors were offering their customers as long as the Net Book Agreement was in place, but the first signs that it was a legislation likely to come under siege were already apparent in the early '90s as Dillon's and Waterstone's, increasingly powerful players in the bookselling game, began a policy of discounting lead titles. This threat was anathema to Peter Kindersley. He knew his phone would never stop ringing if a distributor discovered that a DK title could be bought more cheaply in a bookstore, and for the next few years, until the NBA finally crumbled, he argued passionately for its retention.

It is one thing to run a business where the employees are all handpicked. It is quite another where all but the in-house management are self-elected members of the organisation. And you cannot legislate over who will rise to the top of that membership. The two original proposers of the DK scheme, Charles Dawes and Nigel Byrom, had seen it as a business opportunity: DK books were highly attractive and saleable; the endgame was to make money. Several of the early leaders, those who built up the biggest networks, or down lines, were of a similar opinion. It wasn't of much import to them what they were selling as long as it was commercial – they were more interested in the numbers than the product, and some would have been equally happy flogging lingerie or lavatory brushes. Herein lay the roots of a schism with Peter Kindersley that was never fully resolved. Sure, he saw the business opportunity as clearly as anyone. But he was more interested in the mission of selling books to as broad a franchise as possible, in bringing his carefully crafted home learning tools to a readership way beyond the tiny percentage of the population that ever visits a bookshop, for them to use and enjoy and derive benefits from. There is a messianic element to all home-selling operations, usually impersonated by the founder or CEO of the business, but, like the history of the church, the crusading message can be fragmented when the disciples elect to follow differing creeds.

Thus, by 1992, we had yet another fledgling business on our books, a more complex, unpredictable and time-consuming one than the trade publishing operations. The opportunity was undeniable, but was it manageable with so many other plates spinning in the air? Predictably, DKFL was not welcomed by the trade, and there were early indications of conflict between those running our UK trade sales division, who were dealing directly with the high street, and the arrivistes in Horsham, where DKFL headquarters were based. Peter Kindersley poured scorn on the booksellers' reaction – he was contemptuous of those who blocked his visionary road to progress like a herd of slow-moving cattle. So it was left to the trade sales managers to soothe the ruffled feathers of independent booksellers who had experienced the encroachment of a nest of DKFL distributors in their neighbourhood. Some of the latter occasionally behaved tactlessly, most notably when informing a bookshop proprietor that they could sell the same DK books a lot cheaper. It was impossible to control the behaviour of independent freelancers, and as the network grew, it became harder still, so there was always likely to be a tense relationship with the bookstores who were in the tricky position of wanting DK children's books because they were currently the hot ticket in non-fiction, yet believing their business was going to be eroded by the expansion of the home-selling franchise.

And it was expanding. And it was mostly in the home. A party plan operation. There were those who sold into schools or set up stalls at country fairs and fêtes. But the majority of the business was done by inviting friends and acquaintances round for coffee, displaying a range of tempting books on the table, explaining the risks and rewards (few risks, multiple rewards), and signing them up on the spot. If the attendees brought their children along and witnessed how quickly they were captivated by the books, it was a soft sell. This was in a period of economic uncertainty so the opportunity for generating a second, or just extra, income for the home was hard to resist. And besides the financial benefits, it offered new distributors the chance to expand their circle of acquaintances and grow their own business to a level that could be directly measured according to how much time and effort were put into it. It would be all their own work, they could take pride in it, develop their self-confidence, and at the same time acknowledge to themselves that what they were selling would bring tangible rewards to the lives of others. Unsurprisingly, many of the distributors were young mothers, but there were also a number of teachers who valued the books for their specific support of curriculum activities. Among the men, there were several who had been either laid off or retired, and they ranged from ex-City pinstripes to cab drivers and deli owners. It was a fascinating, eclectic, unpredictable potpourri of the British democracy.

This Dog's a Runner

Summer 1992. The countdown to flotation. The boardroom was awash with papers. Stacks of them, ranged along the walls and loosely scattered on the table. There were bound copies of accounts going back to the beginning of time, files stuffed with author contracts, foreign publishing contracts, summaries of future publishing programmes, warehouse inventories, property leasing agreements, pension schemes, foreign exchange fluctuations, licensing deals, personnel records, bank statements, insurance arrangements, shareholder certificates, catalogues. Every single document that might have relevance to the public flotation of Dorling Kindersley Ltd had been dug out of cupboards, drawers and safes and assembled for the due diligence of the battalion of merchant bankers, stockbrokers, auditors, solicitors, financial advisers and public relations wallahs who would share the responsibility for fattening the bird for market and fattening themselves in the process. Ruddy-cheeked blue bloods in wide-striped shirts and coloured braces brayed at each other across the room about the weekend's house party or the salmon fishing prospects as they riffled through the papers and began drafting the prospectus document. Richard Harman was the chief conductor, ferrying in coffee and sandwiches and handling the barrage of queries they lobbed at him. Other members of the senior management were summoned in turn to give their appraisals of their sector of the business and searchingly questioned on the future prospects.

On the Adult and Children's side we demonstrated the remarkable growth achieved over the past four years, and pointed to a global market that showed no signs of disenchantment with our offerings. In just the last two years Adult turnover had doubled from £19 million to £38 million, while Children's had nearly quadrupled from £7 million to £27 million. The embryo DK list in the US had also sold through above its expected level, and would now be capitalised upon with much fuller and more credible publishing programmes in the coming years. DK Direct demonstrated that theirs was a fail-safe business as nothing was commissioned until it had been tested and underpinned by one of the direct mail giants, and their order book was filling up.

Of the recent start-ups, John Adams played one of the videos adapted from a children's book series in which a duck and her ducklings waddled across the blank white background of the screen to an annoyingly repetitive jingle. This was the DK book look in motion, so the message that it would transfer into this medium was clear enough. Mike Strong displayed the educational kits that would be marketed into schools the following spring. Andrew Heritage from the Cartography division gave a plausible account of how the new digital technology would transform the next generation of maps and geographical databases. Peter Cartwright reported that DKFL had now recruited over 700 distributors, and that plans were now well advanced to extend the business to the US. And Alan Buckingham concluded the presentations with a demonstration of an early DK Multimedia prototype on musical instruments, which held the assembled City folk riveted to their seats. Finally, Peter Kindersley wrapped up the show with his one-man evangelist riff, which culminated in the unveiling of his Total World Domination map on the boardroom wall. The bankers and stockbrokers stared at the map with the kind of religious awe which their forebears must have experienced when contemplating half the world coloured red under the umbrella of the Empire. They were impressed.

'This dog's got £10 written all over it,' said one.

'You could be right, Harry,' said another. 'But not as an initial offering.'

'Reckon it could make the pace early,' said a third. 'Question is, is it a stayer?'

'Yup, you guys will need to do the rounds of the fund managers,' said a fourth, 'and convince them that you aren't Roman candles – you know, rocketing up in a blaze of bright sparks, then crashing back down in the dark. Those people are usually looking for the long-term bets.'

After the presentation the senior management regrouped round the table with Charles Ponsonby, our principal contact from the financial advisers.

'I'd say that was a pretty good start, fellows,' he said. 'You know, you put it across well. I think the message has registered that they might have a flyer here. But we should reduce this to a core team to go round the investment houses. I think three or four max. So who's it going to be?'

'Presumably it has to be led by myself and Richard,' said Peter. 'I'll do the big picture, so to speak. Richard will do the financials. Then I suggest we take Christopher to talk about the publishing and I would advocate having Alan Buckingham along to add some sex appeal with that new media presentation.'

'Sounds good to me,' said Pongo. 'But I'd like to make a couple of suggestions, if you don't mind.'

'Go ahead,' said Peter.

'I know you are first and foremost a creative company with a, shall we say, rather informal house style. But if we are to get these senior players in the fund management business to fork out big time, then they will need to be sure it's not going to some hippy commune in disguise.'

'Blimey, Charles,' said Peter. 'That's a bit rich, I must say. Just because we don't all dress like bankers every day of the week…'

'No, no. I apologise. I just meant that a suit and tie and maybe a haircut or two wouldn't go amiss.'

I looked at Alan. We both knew he was referring to us. It certainly wasn't Richard, who was suited and booted in the image of a group managing director. It wasn't Kindersley either, who could switch seamlessly from creative guru to captain of industry just by changing his clothes. But Alan and I were at the Bohemian end of the scale. I did occasionally put on a tie when I was obliged to meet what we called "grown-ups", but my mop of curly hair and beard still gave me an untamed look. I guessed I had better get it trimmed to satisfy Pongo's concern. As for Alan, it was doubtful that he even possessed a tie. Jeans and casual shirts comprised his habitual gear, while his beard and shoulder length hair lent him the sagacity of a beat poet, the Allen Ginsberg of the electronic age.

'Don't panic, Charles,' he said. 'I've got the message.'

The whole atmosphere at the DK offices in Covent Garden had changed. The usual feverish pressure to meet deadlines on forthcoming titles was now overlaid with a hum of expectation, the sense of a shift in the company's tectonic plates, and the altered landscape which might follow. But the senior people also knew that it could herald a threat to our independence and the freedom of decision making which had characterised our lives until now in the enclosed world of our cottage industry. The cottage was about to become a mansion, and the doors of the mansion would be open to the public as well as to the perpetual scrutiny of the institutional investors, the city analysts and the jackals of the financial press. The financial rewards of a successful public offering would be counterbalanced by the strictures and demands placed upon the directors as we swam in our transparent fishbowl.

The person most in his element during this period was Richard Harman. It had been his long-expressed ambition to take the company to market, and now that it was happening he was relishing every moment. Peter allowed him to orchestrate the whole process and deferred to him on the detail. Richard had hired a legion of helpers; the place was swarming with number crunchers on short-term contracts, many of them Australians eager to earn some extra cash to supplement their wanderings through Europe. They were cheerfully energetic types who worked like demons in the week and drank like demons when it was over. Come six o'clock on a Friday evening the offices would echo to the snapping sounds of tinnies being opened. It all contributed to the atmosphere of barely contained excitement as the company moved closer to the deadline.

Meanwhile we, the elected quartet, were chauffeured through the canyons of the City with our Cazenove minder to make the presentations to the potential shareholders in the institutions. As we became more practised in our routine the chemistry between us became more potent and seemed to find favour with the audience for whom the colourful content and easygoing humour were a welcome change from their usual diet of dourly delivered analysis. Peter impressed because he was so obviously the inspiration and the driver and it was impossible to ignore the fanatical zeal with which he proselytised the company's virtues. Occasionally he became caught up in a web of his own hyperbole and started to wander off message, at which point Richard would politely insert a cautionary rider. Richard himself was completely confident with the numbers and one could detect how even the most sceptical fund managers relaxed into their seats once they realised they were being given the treatment by one of their own kind who clearly knew his business. I followed Richard in the batting order and brought some light relief after the battery of numbers by handing out some of DK's bestselling books and explaining why the qualities of great content, beautifully designed and produced to the highest standards, was a world-beating formula. We had the backlist sales to prove it, and there was no reason why DK shouldn't continue in this vein with groundbreaking new titles. I also slipped in a couple of anecdotes about the eccentricities of some authors which had the desired effect of making the City suits feel vicariously connected to a more glamorous and exotic milieu. Then Alan put on his show. Seated at his Apple Mac, with the images projected onto a flat screen, he dazzled them with examples of how the static two-dimensional pages of a book could be transformed into a moving three-dimensional interactive learning tool on the computer. There were audible intakes of breath from his audience. They were putty in his hands. He didn't need to speak much.

'If I click on here,' he said, scrolling across a photographic cut out of an orchestra, 'then we can play each of the individual instruments.'

'Wow!' they murmured.

'And if I click on two of them, we can hear them playing together.'

'Gosh!' they exclaimed.

'And if you want to learn more about the guitar, about how it features in different forms of music – classical, folk, rock, etc – then we click on this little icon at the side, and bingo, you can choose what you want to hear.'

The plangent notes of Segovia filled the room, then Jimi Hendrix made the walls bulge.

'Fantastic!' they chorused.

They wanted more. This sometimes created a problem as we were on a tight schedule to get round the institutions, but it was also important not to disappoint the investors. So if there was time, Alan gave them glimpses of early prototypes on dinosaurs or the human body. His subtly modulated presentation was undoubtedly the icing on the cake, and the city mandarins were eager to get their slice. The new media would be the clincher in the public offering, moving it up to a higher level.

We were on a roll, but the market wasn't. In fact, almost every City indicator cautioned against flotation that year. The timing was the last thing we had to decide. But then, like the intervention of the soothsayer in *Julius Caesar*, I experienced an unusual augury. On holiday in August in the South of France, in a house full of family and friends, I was seated at dinner one night next to a healer. She knew little about me and nothing about the DK situation. Quite spontaneously, at the end of the meal, she said she had noticed my hands and she was certain that money was going to come my way in the near future. I was astonished.

'Are you sure? Can you, er, be more precise?' I asked, as casually as possible.

'Probably not next month, more likely October,' she replied. 'When the leaves start to turn...'

At the first board meeting after returning from holiday, the question of the timing of the public offering was still high on the agenda.

'So what does everybody think?' said Peter. 'The market

hasn't been too sparky.'

'We just don't know what's going to happen with the market,' said Richard. 'It may stay flat for the rest of the year. On the other hand, there won't be many other companies going public at this time so we could benefit from being out there on our own. It would mean we get a lot more attention.'

'That could be good or bad,' said Robin Holland-Martin, one of the non-executive directors. 'Depends which way up the boat floats. Do we have any other indicators?'

I recounted my holiday experience. They all laughed. But they conceded it was an intriguing twist.

'In that case,' said Peter, 'we could consult Derek and Julia Parker for their prediction.'

Derek and Julia were the authors of some successful astrology titles, which we had published; they always determined the exact minute of the hour of the day when a new book of theirs should be launched for its most propitious conjunction of the stars.

In the end, purely practical matters determined the decision. We all wanted to go for it. September was too soon, and November was reckoned to be too late. A date was fixed for late October.

It was the right call. On the first day of trading the shares jumped from the launch price of 165p to 213p. The initial offering was six times oversubscribed, and this against a background of recession. As Quentin Lumsden of *The Independent* observed, the DK flotation aroused memories of the booming 1980s as investors scrambled for shares. Analysts cited it as the most successful for a company of its size in more

The DK flotation in 1992 was six times oversubscribed, a remarkably successful outcome considering the economy was in a recession.

than fifteen years. The prospectus was described as the 'cutest flotation document the Stock Market had seen'. 'Resounding success for DK share offer' read one headline; 'Eyewitness to a fortune' proclaimed another. We were definitely flavour of the month.

When I look back at the succeeding months of that year it seemed like Christmas had come early and just kept going. The public offering created widespread interest in the national press as well as in the trade journals, much of it focused on the rise and rise of Peter Kindersley, who was now in the mega-bucks bracket and the predictable target of every imaginable charitable organisation. The Kindersley family was profiled in Sunday supplements and style magazines with pictures of the small back room in South London where the great enterprise had begun, and any description of Peter was invariably accompanied by 'genius' or 'visionary' or 'master mind', and sometimes all three in the same sentence. He was photographed in the boardroom with a dazzling array of DK bestsellers in the background. He was photographed on the steps of the building, beneath the company sign. Occasionally he was photographed with Richard and myself on either side as his two lieutenants. But this was basically for variety. Peter was rightly the focal point of the financial reporters' attention because he was the primary architect of the business, and he was the focal point of the gossipy press because publishing was sexy and he was very rich. He was unlikely, however, to satisfy the hunger of the scandal-mongering diarists. The ascetic lifestyle characterised by yoga and herbal tea infusions was infertile ground for those looking for tales of unbridled decadence, financial scams, rent boy kiss-and-tells or lines of coke snorted off the butt of a lap dancer.

The canonisation of Peter Kindersley was expected, and accepted, by the rest of the company, many of whom, thanks to his exceptional generosity with the share options scheme, now had a stake in the business. The longest-serving staff had done very well out of the flotation. It was as though we had been blessed with a life-changing windfall.

The company hosted a party to celebrate the flotation. The only depressing coda to the evening was that Charles Ponsonby, who had worked with the utmost diligence on our behalf and played a major role in the success of the offering, had been let go by BZW as soon as the job was done. The cold steel of a City axe. But we subsequently employed his services when he set up his own financial PR business.

Later that evening I walked down to the river. Leaning against the railings, I smoked a last cigarette and watched the dark waters as they slid by. This has been an extraordinary journey, I mused. I can't believe how lucky I was to have been in the right place at the right time and chosen by Peter to share the ride. But can we sustain it? Will it all be utterly changed henceforth? Will the spirit of creative endeavour be nurtured, or will it be smothered beneath a blizzard of numbers?

I flicked the butt into the river. It glowed for a second as it fell, then vanished on the tide.

Showing What Others Only Tell

The all-singing, all-dancing appeal of the embryo CD-ROMs may have been the jewel that dazzled the institutional investors at the flotation but we had another gem in the locker on the books side that we weren't quite ready to unveil.

A couple of years earlier, before the management moved into the grander premises next door at 7–8 Henrietta Street, we had met with Pierre Marchand of Gallimard in the windowless bunker of No 9. The *Eyewitness* children's series was well and truly launched around the world and now on a steady production line of eight titles a year. The purpose of the meeting was to plot the next revolution, to find the new over-arching concept that would foment astonishment among our peers and partners.

Gallimard and Dorling Kindersley had both arrived at the same point in our researches. We were living in a highly visual age with a growing population of relatively wealthy people who had the opportunity and desire to explore the world and enjoy its cultural treasures. Yet none of the offerings on display in the travel sections of bookstores reflected those visual glories. There were purely cultural guides like the Michelin *Green Guides*; there were the full-colour populist APA guides, illustrated with picture postcard-style photographs; and there was a raft of unillustrated guides. But there weren't any that led you round a city by the hand and allowed you to glimpse its heritage.

The tag line adopted for the *Eyewitness* children's series was "The books that show you what others only tell you." We believed that we could harness that same principle in creating a new generation of travel guides.

It was one of those brainstorming sessions that are worth a hundred days of routine desk work and make the milieu of publishing seem like the best place in the world to be. We began with the imagined arrival in a country of a foreign visitor – at an airport, railway terminus or seaport. What is the first thing he or she needs to know? Answer: how to use a public telephone. Solution: photograph one. (This pre-dated the era of the ubiquitous mobile phone.) Which coins in the local currency do you need to insert? Show them. Do you insert them before or after lifting the receiver? Annotate the photograph to show the sequence. And so on to the next task: buying a ticket for a bus or train or subway ride into the city. Photograph the machines and the coins. The traveller reaches the city centre, stands in Trafalgar Square or St Peter's Square or Times Square. Create a three-dimensional map with the key buildings highlighted so it is easy to look up and orient oneself. Show the typical dishes of the country for the traveller's first experience of local cuisine. Explode with cutaway artwork the insides of St Paul's or the Musée d'Orsay or the Uffizi so that it works as a progressive guide as one walks round the cathedral or the gallery, and highlight the must-see works of art if the visitor has only an hour or two to spare. So it went on. We knew that we had something in this approach. It was exhilarating. This could be the beginning of another brilliant joint venture.

Pierre Marchand left for Paris. But, unlike the intensive collaboration which we had pursued together to hammer out the original *Eyewitness* concept, he declined to make further contact. At the next book fair, we asked him about the travel guides. He replied that he was working on the proposal, but he seemed evasive. Months went by. Finally, we cornered him and asked to see his work in progress. He produced a large pile of dummy presentation boards which, while showing evidence of the cultural emphasis we had discussed, seemed to ignore the practicalities of survival in a city. Peter Kindersley pushed him to elaborate on his plans.

'Are you prepared to work with us on these guides as we originally assumed or are you going to develop them on your own?'

Pierre smiled and shrugged his shoulders in that typically Gallic gesture of avoiding a difficult issue.

A few months later we discovered that he had sold the English language rights to his old comrade, David Campbell at Everyman. This decision galvanised us into action.

'Right,' said Peter. 'That settles it. We are going to create our own guides and we'll now be in competition with Gallimard.'

It was a bizarre and unexpected turn of events. Later I discovered the probable reason for it. Not long after the *Eyewitness* children's series had been launched with outstanding success in France, Pierre Marchand was invited on to a prestigious cultural TV programme to discuss them. At some point in the interview he was asked why these books had been created in England and not in France. Of course this was an arrow to the heart of his Breton pride, and from that moment it seemed that he had to defend the honour of France at all costs and prove to the world that Gallimard was once again capable of producing a global blockbusting series. I never heard this from Pierre directly, but it is what I have concluded from having the story relayed to me by one of his colleagues.

So it came to pass that the Entente Cordiale became the Entente Competitif and the two most expensive series of travel guides in the history of publishing were produced in parallel and fought for the same footholds with co-edition partners around the world. They were of similar format, similarly priced, and targeted the same readership. Gallimard, who had a head start from Pierre's months of secret development work, raced ahead, commissioning a swathe of titles, including, somewhat to our disbelief, seven volumes on Brittany alone. Plainly Pierre was not going to allow even one square centimetre of his native region to be overlooked. DK moved more circumspectly; we concentrated on perfecting the details of the concept and then, for two years, we poured all our efforts into delivering the two thousand odd pages which would constitute the *Eyewitness Travel Guides* to the "Big

Four" – London, Paris, New York, and Rome.

I know one thing for sure. We couldn't have embarked upon this series earlier than we did, and if I had asked in recent years for £2 million to spend on the first four titles of a new travel series, it would have been met with derision. The combination of the good luck we had with Bill Gates's investment and the subsequent influx of cash from the flotation enabled us to ride the development costs without major discomfort. And these factors enabled me to keep the accountants off my back while we threw our energies into selling the series internationally, promoting it to the bookselling communities in the UK and the US, and marketing it to a public previously unaccustomed to paying £15 and more for a travel guide.

Every few months Peter Gill, who had joined DK after the flotation as CFO, parked his towering frame beside my desk and fixed me with an inquisitorial glare.

'So when do you reckon these travel guides are going to move into the black, Christopher?' he boomed.

'Just think Japanese, Peter. This could be a great business. Any normal reference publisher would give them seven years to break even.'

He wasn't deflected by my bluster.

'You estimate that we might start seeing a return on our investment by the end of the century? Is that what you are saying?'

'That's rather a doom-laden way of looking at it,' I replied. 'I'm prepared to bet money that it will be much sooner than we anticipate.'

The grounds for my optimism were not ill-founded. I had

taken it on myself to travel the world with the international sales team to negotiate the rights to the guides. We had pitched high and hard. The cost of entry was jaw dropping to some, but so was the fear that if they didn't pay up to join the club, they might be missing out on a very lucrative line of business in the future. This sales strategy proved effective. While some major publishing houses, often long-term allies of Pierre Marchand, were torn between their loyalty to Gallimard and their regard for the DK offerings, there was always another house to turn to if the decision went against us. There was only one significant casualty. In Japan, Dohosha were hugely cash-rich from a run of very successful partworks and they had invested significantly in other DK series. In fact, at one point they approached us to ask if they could be our exclusive publisher in Japan, an offer we were wise to decline as they subsequently over-reached themselves and then became the victims of the economic downturn in that market. But the probable trigger of their demise was their indecision over whether to choose the Gallimard guides or the *Eyewitness* guides, an indecision so profound they could only resolve it by opting for the worst possible solution, namely to acquire both of them.

When the first four *Eyewitness Travel Guides* were launched in September 1993, we were head-to-head with the UK launch of the Gallimard series under the Everyman banner. The critics reviewed them together as a new, pricey, but glamorous phenomenon in this publishing category. What was best about the Gallimard guides were exactly those romantic elements Pierre Marchand had brought to the *Eyewitness* children's books – cultural sophistication and stylishness. They

With over 50 million copies sold, the *Eyewitness Travel Guides* have become world leaders in the category, and the most profitable line in the company's business.

contained more about the artistic traditions of a place than ours did, they sometimes used striking silver, gold or black backgrounds, they had a feeling of calculated richness. The *Eyewitness* guides, on the other hand, possessed the pure clarity of the Kindersley work ethic, but what they may have lacked in French finesse, they gained in organisation and practical application. The travellers who could afford both guides to Paris, for example, would probably enjoy reading about literary life on the Left Bank in the Gallimard edition over breakfast, but would of necessity take the *Eyewitness* volume to accompany them around the sights of the Sixième.

In hindsight one could say it was perhaps a pity we couldn't have combined our efforts as originally envisaged and jointly produced a series more striking than our individual efforts. But national pride and the Channel had divided us. Over the years it became apparent that *Eyewitness* was the winner; by the time I retired from DK it was the most profitable business in the whole of Penguin UK, and one of the brands most easily identified with DK around the world. Alas for Pierre Marchand, the huge investment that Gallimard had placed in his dream project may ultimately have contributed to his departure from that company. When he moved to Hachette, we met up once again to brainstorm a new concept in information books for the young. Soon after came the shocking news of his death. I still think of him as a genius of illustrated publishing and remember him with affection and admiration.

The worldwide success of the *Eyewitness Travel Guides*, and the other series that followed, owes a huge debt to Douglas

Amrine who became the publisher of the travel division at the outset and, apart from a brief intermission, has remained at its head ever since. He is one of those "good" Americans of whom Oscar Wilde approved: when they die, they go to Paris. He might have become a full-time classical musician – he first came to Europe to play the famous organ in a Dutch church, and he still gives harpsichord recitals. But the need to make ends meet led him into editing, and ultimately to his position on the guides, where his combined attributes of cultural sensitivity, canniness, determination and good sense have ensured the standards of excellence have been maintained. At the beginning the guides were all created in house at a cost in excess of £1,500 per page. This was clearly unsustainable. Now, to save origination spend and overheads, Douglas has well-trained teams around the world to help compile them to his exacting specifications, including a sizeable DK unit in Delhi which is contributing significantly to the annual output.

The fanfare that greeted the launch of the *Eyewitness Travel Guides* provided a fitting conclusion to a year that had begun in February with DK being awarded the accolade of Publisher of the Year at the annual Nibbies (the book trade's Oscars). But that honour was largely retrospective. It seems that one of the factors appreciated by the industry was that we had been bold enough to go for a public flotation. This was something no other publishing company had done for some time and it was felt it paved the way for others to follow.

Publishing Fundamentals

Public flotation can change the dynamics of a company, especially a creative one. With hindsight, I am not convinced that becoming a plc is a wise move for any business built on the continuous generation of fresh ideas and dependent on the lottery of a notoriously unpredictable marketplace. Will the sales increase next year? Will the profits grow? Will the margins improve? Will the overheads be contained? During the amazing uninterrupted surf ride we had enjoyed over the previous four years, such questions, while raised every time the annual budget was compiled, were never taxing enough to keep one awake at night. Now they were a matter of quarterly scrutiny by analysts and fund managers, keen to be reassured that the flotation message was still to be trusted and that their bets on the share price had been on a thoroughbred and not on a donkey.

For the first twelve months of Dorling Kindersley's status as a listed company we were relatively untroubled by the close attentions of the City's inspectorate. The first interim report, and six months later, the first full year's accounts confirmed that market confidence had not been misplaced. Turnover for the year ending June 30, 1993 was £87 million (up from £70 million) and profits were up by £2 million to £9.6 million. The established businesses were continuing to show handsome growth, with strong frontlist titles and, more importantly, a 46 per cent increase in backlist revenues. The new businesses were starting to achieve momentum. In the US, DK Inc's revenues had risen to £13.7 million from a standing start less than two years earlier, and we had also hired John Sargent as CEO in succession to Steven Sussmann, who had been let go (summoned to a breakfast with Kindersley that would have mildewed his muesli).

In October the shares stood at 351p, just a year after they were floated at 165p. The red tops made much of Peter Kindersley's shareholding, trying to build a rags-to-riches story from the casual jobs he had taken in his student days – he had at some point cleaned offices and worked as a stoker at Battersea Gas Works. On this occasion *The Sun* headline read: 'PETE CLEANS UP £50M IN A YEAR – Books make Mr Mopp's Fortune.'

The euphoria didn't last. In December reality kicked in like a Thai boxer. The Tiptree distribution operation run by Random House in the UK had become dysfunctional to the extent that our projected sales for the Christmas period, and therefore our figures for the full year, were seriously mauled. In addition, the teaching packs supplied by DK Education were experiencing a shortfall in sales to schools. We had to issue a profit warning, which caused the share price to slide, followed by another a fortnight later when Peter despatched Richard Harman for 'losing interest in the business'. Rod Hare, by now in the role of COO, was promoted to MD in Richard's place. The share price dipped to 221p. It was a bleak, disruptive time. The *Daily Mail* sarcastically suggested that as a publisher of self-help manuals we should try a new one: 'How to Lose your Managing Director, Row with your Distributor and Forecast Lower Profits without Upsetting Shareholders.'

The distribution crisis also badly affected the DKFL business as customers either received no books at all or were supplied with ones they hadn't ordered. It became farcical. The export rep to the Middle East opened a carton in front of one of his Egyptian clients, but instead of the anticipated selection of books he was confronted by the bottom half of a pair of pyjamas. The pressure from the City meant that it was hard to find the humour in the situation, and the atmosphere between DK and Random House became rancorous and vitriolic before the dispute was eventually passed into the hands of the lawyers. ('Shall I write them a letter I wouldn't like to receive?' said Giles Cunningham, our smart, engaging and very laid-back legal director.) It was just about possible to calculate a figure on our lost earnings through the bookstores but almost impossible to measure the downturn in DKFL revenues because one of the immediate side-effects of a distribution failure in a direct-selling operation is that the self-employed distributors migrate away from the business like a flock of starlings. If they have built up a network and then leave their down line beached from lack of product, the whole pyramid can collapse. It is a commercial enterprise dependent almost entirely on the elements of confidence and trust. And those two elements are difficult to rebuild without the hard physical evidence that what they order can be guaranteed to arrive. We faced an uphill battle to bring the year in without too much damage.

No doubt word of these distribution troubles spread across the Atlantic when the fledgling DKFL operation was hatching in the US. We had recruited Alan Luce, a long-term veteran of Tupperware, to head the business, and he was busy persuading former colleagues to join him in the Orlando headquarters while putting out feelers across the States for experienced networkers who could build downlines in geographical pockets around the country. In many ways it proved an easier sell than in the UK. There were ready-made disciples in the burgeoning home-schooling fraternity who saw DK books as the ideal tool for family learning. And there was a significant underbelly of the population who recognised the advantages those books would confer on their children in the race to be the brightest and the best. Many of the recruited distributors, particularly in the Midwest, approached the business with the same fundamentalist zeal that they brought to their adopted religion. It wasn't long before they were expressing strong views about the kind of books they wanted to see on our list, and indeed about others they would prefer we never published. Sex books, for example, had become a hot ticket for DK in the US trade, which caused Peter Kindersley some embarrassment with these vocal distributors, but there was no escaping either his own inheritance – he had been the art director on *The Joy of Sex* while at Mitchell Beazley – nor his own insistence on creating new, and raunchier, bonking manuals for the American mainstream. There was also the thorny issue of evolution, which unsurprisingly featured prominently in our pre-history titles but was deemed pagan propaganda by those for whom the first chapter of Genesis is the truth.

As with the UK business, the US DKFL membership wanted books produced exclusively for them. There was a stronger case for doing this than in the UK as there was the potential, if the recruitment took off, for the numbers in the US to be very significant. But it was a tough job persuading one of our editorial teams that we should originate a title on creationism. This generated tensions in the company, not least because Peter reflected the ambivalence of his position as the commercial driving force of DK as a business and as the semi-deified figurehead of the DKFL mission. To try and forge some common ground a bunch of senior people on the creative side flew across the Atlantic to meet up with the leaders of the DKFL network and discuss future publishing ideas.

(I have combined several such meetings into a semi-fictional scenario.)

Scene: Gloomy function room of typical Midwestern hotel.

Cast: DK editorial/design personnel; Alan Luce; DKFL leading distributors (names and characteristics changed).

The DK contingent was ranged in chairs across the podium, the distributors in the front rows of the auditorium. Alan Luce introduced them in turn, with ringing endorsements of the number of people they had recruited and the revenues they had generated over a remarkably short space of time.

'These folks,' he added in his stentorian tones, 'are on the road to the kind of substantial rewards of which most of us can only dream, and they should be an example to all of us of what can be achieved through dedication and hard work.'

We all applauded.

Apart from the virtues of dedication and industry, I found it hard to discern what else these leaders of the business shared in common. There was Cindy, from Seattle, a goofy-looking young woman with protruding teeth who had abandoned a lowly clerking position to take up the DKFL baton; Bruce, a huge Native American from Oklahoma, recently retired from pro football; Mary, a sweet but quietly determined teacher from Phoenix; Chuck, a big cheese from the industrial north, now retired to Florida; Ellie May, a genteel blonde of indeterminate years from Dallas, who might have stepped out of a Tennessee Williams play yet whose apparently distracted air concealed a steely will; Pearl, the big momma of the group (physically and literally – she had nine children), from St Louis; Karen, a business-like former bookseller from Minneapolis; and Clem, a scrawny lay preacher from the Carolinas whose expression was so sour, I wondered how he had managed to recruit so many people. Maybe they were all members of his congregation, threatened by the fires of hell if they didn't sign up.

'Right, folks,' said Alan, clapping his hands enthusiastically. 'We want you to tell our friends here from the UK what you think of the books and what else you might be wanting them to create for us.'

Clem was the first to speak.

'I'd like something clarified about the company's publishing philosophy,' he droned, looking as though he had swallowed a porcupine doused in lemon juice. 'There's a title you produced, the *Eyewitness Handbook of Fossils*, which is proving very popular with the folks in my neck of the woods. But let me tell you this. I would be selling ten times the number of copies I sell at present if it weren't for one small picture, and on that account I'm requesting that you find a way to remove the offending image.'

'Can you show me which picture you are referring to?' I asked.

'Sure. I have it right here,' said Clem, handing over the book. He had tagged a page from the introductory chapter, which explained the process of carbon dating and captioned an image of a fossil that could be identified as coming from some 50 million years ago.

'Er, so what exactly is the problem with this?' I enquired, somewhat disingenuously, knowing full well what was in store.

'It's from before the Book of Genesis,' said Clem, smacking his puckered lips, 'so it ain't true. You're propagating a falsehood with this misinformation.'

'But, excuse me, this is a scientifically proven fact,' I replied, as evenly as possible. 'It isn't a theory, it's a precise measurement of time.'

'If God hadn't wanted us to find these fossils in the ground, he wouldn't have put them there,' said Clem with the triumphant air of someone playing a trump card. 'And

God couldn't have put them there before he created the world and all that there is in it. Which, as you know, is in the first chapter of the Bible.'

I bit my lip and counted to ten. I needed to keep my cool. The atmosphere in the room was tense. They were waiting for my response, my colleagues alongside hoping I wouldn't let the side down, the distributors curious to see how this would resolve itself. It was clear from their body language that a number were supportive of the preacher's viewpoint. Yet there were others, I could detect, who did not agree with this intervention, and some who would oppose it as vehemently as I did. This was tricky. If I refused outright to countenance Clem's argument, I knew that Peter Kindersley would be swamped by angry emails. This was one of the difficulties of a business in which the participants were not employees of the company yet each expected individual treatment. Peter had possibly made a mistake in making himself so open to their

A popular subject in the American heartland but some claimed DK would have sold more copies if all references to carbon dating had been removed. A fundamental truth?

responses. If twenty emails appeared in his in-box supporting one view he would in his mind multiply that to the scale of a mass protest and conclude that the business was being undermined. His natural reaction in these circumstances was to give priority to whatever they asked. But the senior DK managers were equally adamant that the integrity of their editorial standards be maintained. And there were the practicalities of book production to be considered. It would be economic folly to print two editions of the book, one with the evolutionary science removed and one with it retained. The costs would double. Besides, how would you identify which was which? Would you catalogue one as the Genesis Edition and the other as the Darwin Edition? It was ridiculous.

I decided we had to play for time. The DKFL network was in its infancy. It would be unwise to be confrontational at this stage, and in any case they would see it as the arrogant Brits thinking they know best.

Eventually I said, 'I understand your viewpoint, Clem. And I appreciate that you can't remove the offending page without devaluing the book. So we will look at the possibility of publishing the next edition without that particular image, although I don't feel it right that we should remove the content about how scientists research the past.'

It was a compromise that seemed to lift the tension in the room. Clem was mollified, though only partially. He carried the book back to his seat with a marginally less acid expression. But it wasn't a closed issue.

'I'd like to know how you are going to treat this question in your children's books,' said Karen, who was evidently on the Darwinian bench. 'The Fossils guide is a family book, but what about how we teach the very young about the origins of everything? I hope it's going to be an open-minded approach.'

'I'm with Clem,' said Pearl in her big deep voice. 'If what the Bible says is good enough for the Reverend, then it sure is good enough for me.'

'Sorry, but I'm with Karen,' said Mary. 'As teachers we are obliged to offer an open book, not a closed one. We are there to help the young understand the world better and we won't be performing our duty if we deny them knowledge that is available to others.'

'Ah do believe there's so much prejudice in the world that we should do everything in our powers to avoid it being an issue,' added Ellie May in her Blanche Dubois voice.

'Hell, yes,' said Chuck, who was more interested in the numbers of books he could sell rather than what was in them. 'Just give us titles that ain't got no controversial topics in 'em so we can go into any home and not even have to think about what's suitable or not.'

'Me personally,' said Bruce, 'I'd like to see some books that reflect all cultures. See, many tribes of my people had different stories for how the world began which they handed down through the ages, passing the legends along from parents to children, and these days those stories are in danger of being lost or forgotten. But they believed in those legends as much as some of you folks believe in the Book of Genesis and there ain't nothing dishonest in that. So I would like you to publish a book with all the different versions of the beginnings of everything from all around the world. It'd be real interesting.'

'I agree,' said Cindy. 'We need to learn about other peoples in the world as much as we need to learn about the different peoples in the United States. The world's getting smaller all the time and we risk our kids growing up in isolation if they aren't given the tools to understand other cultures.'

We were grateful for these revealing contributions from the senior distributors. It made our job easier in that we could appreciate the diversity of this audience. At the same time it made it more difficult because what pleased one would offend another. It was like preparing a buffet menu that would satisfy carnivores, vegetarians, macrobiotics, carb addicts, protein fixators, pineapple fetishists and nut allergists, not to mention the strict dietary requirements of the religious persuasions.

'The plain fact is, Christopher,' said Alan Luce as if in summary, 'you need to avoid the obviously contentious. But let me tell you this. These folks here are going to sell many more books for kids than for adults. A ratio of ten to one, in my opinion. All the young mothers you see here will be inviting other young mothers into their homes and what will they want to buy? Right. Books for little Jack or little Jill. You should concentrate on bringing them a whole library of books for the preschool child, because that's where we are going to go gangbusters on the sales front.'

Peter Kindersley was waiting for me when I flew back to London on the red-eye. Before I could change my clothes and grab a cup of coffee, he had gripped me by the elbow and steered me into the boardroom.

'How did you get on?' he asked impatiently. His hands had a slight tremor and there was a yellowish tinge to his eyes. I was familiar with these early morning symptoms – they usually signalled stormy weather.

'Did you agree to what they wanted?' he went on before I could answer. 'There isn't any argument about it, you know. In that kind of business the customer is always right.'

He had obviously assumed that I hadn't carried out his mission as he would have wished. Or maybe a distributor had put in a weaselly phone call.

'Peter, we reached what I believe to be a compromise that leaves everybody reasonably satisfied,' I said. 'There are very strong objections among the editors to bowing down before what they consider to be ignorant religious hokum – and I can't say I disagree with them – but we can make subtle changes which will mollify the fundamentalists and not impair the integrity of the content. It is bound to cost us a bit in production terms and it will surprise our foreign co-publishers but if we can hold everyone together there won't be any losers.'

Peter looked slightly less wound up, though he still hadn't relaxed his grip on my elbow.

'But what about creating titles exclusively for the DKFL distributors? That's what they want.'

'Well, we can when there are enough of them to justify the origination costs. At the moment the print runs just wouldn't be big enough.'

'To hell with that,' he snapped. 'This is the old chicken and egg situation. If we don't give them the books they want now, then they'll never recruit the number of distributors we need to generate big revenues. You've got to think ahead. If DKFL works as I believe it can, it will be far bigger than the rest of our business. We could have hundreds of thousands of people selling our books in just a few years. Then we can forget about the trade and all the miseries of trying to get our books promoted in the front of bookstores.'

'Yes, Peter, I know. But I believe we can grant them their wishes without straying into contentious subject matter. Basically, they need preschool books, simple concepts beautifully executed. Most of the distributors are mothers, and many are people who didn't grow up in homes that had books. They are the real crusaders because they want their kids to have the advantages that they never had.'

'Yes, I'm well aware of that. In fact, I have been saying as much all along. But we have to provide them with their own exclusive range that can't be found in a bookstore, so they aren't competing on price.'

'We are going to do just that,' I said. 'Linda's completely on board. And she is coming up with a plush character that will be all theirs. They went crazy when she presented the idea.'

'Brilliant,' said Peter, his body language now somewhere near normal. 'Show me when she's developed it. And make sure it's an animal that will be accepted internationally. I want to take DKFL further afield as soon as possible.'

'It's a teddy bear. You can't go wrong with a bear if he's lovable enough, especially in the US. He will be a sweet, biddable, engaging and heart-warming character.'

'Well, just make sure she writes a story about the bear's adventures on Noah's Ark. That will help settle the Reverend Clem's acidity level.'

Click and Point

The acidity level of the City analysts still remained high when we posted the full year results to June 1994. Our best efforts to compensate for the distribution problem in the UK had not been enough to salvage the pre-tax profits, which dipped to £9 million. On the other hand, we had managed to increase turnover by over 20 per cent to £107 million, largely thanks to the burgeoning overseas sales and the steady rise of the US publishing company. But we still had to endure the gimlet scrutiny of the city analysts, who sat taking notes in the boardroom as Peter Kindersley, Rod Hare, Peter Gill and myself scrolled through the PowerPoint and determinedly introduced positives whenever a negative needed balancing. Sometimes it felt as if we were swimmers treading water, and the analysts were swift in their arrest. The figures were a disappointment, and the questions rained down.

'We were expecting ten per cent growth in profits. Why hasn't that happened?'

'Do you have any major bestsellers lined up for next year?'

'When is DK Multimedia expected to make a profit?'

'Are the DK Family Library start-ups growing as fast as predicted?'

'Have you got the overheads under control?'

'What is the problem with deliveries from the warehouse, and when will it be solved?'

The four of us were prepared for this interrogation and we batted back our pre-rehearsed answers as confidently as we could. But it was tough going, and it got worse when we had to repeat the presentation to the financial journalists who were markedly less polite in their quest for the slip of the tongue that would give them a scabrous headline.

'Welcome to the real world, chaps,' said Charles Ponsonby afterwards. 'You put on a brave show, but I don't need to tell you that they aren't happy bunnies. The share price may take a pasting.'

Peter Kindersley was irritable, as he frequently was at any hint of criticism.

'Who cares about the share price, Charles? It's just a number in the newspaper.'

'A great many people care, Peter, particularly those who put so much faith in the company at the flotation.'

'Well, if they've got any sense, they will know that we are still in the process of expanding, and having to pay for that expansion as we go, and this isn't a quick fix business. They should be looking to the future.'

'Sure. But they worry when a company starts to slide backwards.'

'Then you can tell them that I am prepared to buy more shares myself to prove my commitment to achieving our goals.'

He was even more annoyed when Peter Gill brought him the evening paper with a derogatory headline on its City page.

'And I don't care what these idiots say either,' he said, screwing up the paper and chucking it into the bin. 'What do they know? They just want a cheap sensation to sell their rag. Tomorrow nobody will remember what it was about.'

None of the other directors believed he didn't care. His emotional reaction was a cover up. This didn't bode well. Since the beginning of the company Peter had never been publicly subjected to the judgment of others. He had ruled the roost secure in his belief that it was his company and he was going to do what he believed to be the right thing for it and anyone who disagreed could go bowl a hoop in the park. Now, although he was the major shareholder, it was no longer entirely his to play with as he liked. This made him both more ill-tempered and more determined, and when he was in this mood he didn't cushion the staff from the fallout. He dumped on them.

That first downturn in profits was a harsh lesson for everyone. The company had enjoyed such a remarkable winning streak over the previous years that it came as a shock when it suffered a blip. The growth had been spontaneous and organic as our innovatively designed titles established Dorling Kindersley as the leader in its field and each year new markets overseas opened up to embrace them. We hadn't bothered much with excessively detailed annual budgets. The basic premise surrounding a new title had been: if it's a good idea and if people want it, then let's do it, and never mind too much about what it costs to make because the sales would recoup that in short order. As long as there were enough new good ideas, supported by the growing backlist, then it was odds-on that they would outstrip the previous year's sales. It seemed as easy as falling off a log, and the steep ascendancy of the annual sales graph had meant that the company had never been seriously embarrassed.

Now it was different. There were financial rules and regulations to be observed, and three non-executive directors sat on the board to make sure that they were. The number of accountants in house had seemingly doubled. The annual budget was a prosaically itemised line-by-line projection of the revenues which every single title would generate in every single market in every single month, to be methodically scrutinised on a monthly basis, analysed and reported on in mind-numbing meetings of bum-numbing duration.

There wasn't, however, a major issue with the established book divisions, which were still predicting impressive global expansion. The more pressing concerns were with the uncertain rates of growth in the two DKFL territories, and with the vast quantities of cash which the Multimedia Division was hoovering up in its admirable, but costly, pursuit of the brightest and best products in the new world of CD-ROMs. This was uncharted territory. Every smart producer in charge of a title in development wanted to add another winning feature, another "what if you clicked on that and it opened another dialog box which in turn accessed another window into the library of cyberspace information?" It seemed that every time a work in progress was reviewed, particularly if Peter Kindersley was present, an extra bell or whistle was added to sex it up. This made it almost impossible to arrive at a sustainable budget for a title. But there were two battles to be won. The first, as with the DK book model, was to create top-of-the-range material for a global audience. And there was no doubt that this was proving successful. The prototypes of the CD-ROMs were so captivating that the international sales people were able to persuade the foreign language customers to stump up the high cost of entry which we demanded of our partners. As with the travel guides, it was a case of signing up or risking being excluded from a potentially enriching club.

The second battle was with Microsoft. Even though we had resisted their overtures to acquire us, and they had then become semi-benevolent minority shareholders, there was never any kinship between the two companies. The cultures were dissimilar for one thing, and it was apparent that Microsoft had never really forgiven DK for holding on to the rights to *The Way Things Work* and developing the CD-ROM ourselves rather than handing it over to them. It was, after all, the reason they had walked into our offices in the first place. Their assumption that we would roll over, wave our legs in the air, and hand over all our content to be developed by them on a multimedia platform was seriously misguided. Peter Kindersley's insistence on DK building up and owning its content was not so that it could be readily exploited by others. The advent of a new publishing platform was to him an opportunity to be seized. Delivering illustrated reference in a different medium, but bearing all the distinctive design hallmarks he had so assiduously cultivated, would expand the brand. He acknowledged that Microsoft would have the advantage of superior technical know-how but doubted that they could bring quality design to their products. So the DK Multimedia division set about recruiting the necessary software expertise while packing its editorial and design ranks with talented émigrés from the book divisions. This in turn created paranoia in Seattle, from Bill Gates down, as they realised that, instead of being a compliant vassal in their empire, DK could eventually become a competitor. The key differential was content, which DK possessed and Microsoft did not. They might be able to manufacture the fastest car on the planet but they didn't have access to oil. Their response was to become defensive, and protective of their technical know-how. But their reluctance to share this with us didn't seem to hamper the Multimedia team, who stormed ahead at breakneck speed, determined to be among the first to plant a distinctive flag on this terra nova.

The first tranche of titles was officially launched in the autumn of 1994 with a glitzy party and bags of hoopla. The response was terrific, every CD-ROM reviewed and garlanded with multiple stars. Nobody doubted their quality and nobody questioned their appeal to the targeted audience. The big issue was price. It was a marketplace without frontiers. There was no issue with the cost of manufacturing; the difficulty was how to gauge what people would pay for this new medium, and whether it would be enough to recoup the high level of origination spend. Herein lay the seeds of a marketing nightmare. Unlike a book, whose production values can be quickly measured from a cursory flick through the pages, a disc is a disc is a disc. There was nothing to indicate to the browser in the high street electronic chains which CD-ROM might offer the real value-for-money content, no marker to distinguish the bog standard baseline treatment of a subject, costing perhaps a few thousand pounds to produce, from the multi-faceted version, such as DK was creating, costing hundreds of thousands of pounds. It became the battle of the boxes. Invest in the cardboard packaging surrounding the disc, bulk it up and allow yourself space on its front, back and sides to sell the content – though this was essentially a war without resolution, because anyone can claim their product is the ultimate experience. Only the recommendations of the reviews and/or an actual demo could serve as reliable guides to the consumer. In the end, it didn't work as a high street business.

The quality of the DK CD-ROMs and videos was universally acknowledged, which made it all the more dispiriting that their success was so short-lived.

And, as is common with TV sets, computers, and other new wave technology, the launch prices were unsustainable. DK's CD-ROMs traded initially at £99 in the UK and $99 in the US, basically finger-in-the-air figures. Within a few years they were selling at a fifth of that, sometimes less.

In many respects it was a tragedy that the multimedia business proved to be such a short-lived episode in publishing history. If it had been allowed to germinate to its full flowering, it might have had a transforming effect on the organised dissemination of information, particularly to the young. But the tidal wave of the internet closed over it so rapidly and so pervasively that the soil in which it was growing was washed away. A vital educational tool was lost to the pace of change; well ordered, accessible knowledge within a single format gave way to random unfiltered information. There was no way to sandbag what at the start of the decade had been the future and by the end of it was the past.

During those years in the 1990s in which DK's Multimedia Division enjoyed its place in the spotlight, it fully deserved the acclaim it received. The teams working on the various CD-ROMs, most of which were adaptations or new versions of popular DK book subjects, applied all the traditional company production values of beauty, usefulness, authority and global appeal to the concept, and then pushed it to the limits of the available technology, adding movement and music and interactive elements to a previously static world. Plus fun. Lots of fun. It was a wonderful exposition of the art of the possible.

We were all convinced that the educational value of the CD-

ROMs in the home was their prize asset. This was reinforced by the numbers which the DKFL distributors racked up as the titles became available. As time went by, the party plan effect of bringing DK books into someone's home was proving increasingly successful. A child could be swiftly pacified with a volume on dinosaurs or knights in armour. But slip a CD-ROM on such subjects into the home computer and the effect was mesmerising. He or she became instantly engaged, and quickly familiar with the navigation tools. It wasn't difficult to predict in those days that CD-ROMs might become the real drivers of that business. Inevitably they were being sold at a heavy discount to their original price, but it was possible to calculate that a volume-driven operation could over time prove lucrative.

During this peak period of production on all fronts, DK Vision created a compelling series of videos based on the *Eyewitness* children's series, in which wild animals could be seen crawling, slithering, prowling, stalking, chasing, swimming and flying through the rooms of a virtual museum before emerging into their natural habitats. It was adopted for broadcast by the BBC Natural History Unit, but unfortunately – on the "not-invented-here" principle, we suspected – was relegated to some obscure kiss-of-death time slot and so never reached the audience it deserved and whom it might have captivated. One thing was for sure – the trademark DK look was everywhere to be seen, in print, on disc, on tape. It was close to becoming a brand.

The Nun's Tale

As a creator of illustrated reference works for an international readership it was critical for Dorling Kindersley to stay close to its network of markets around the world. One of the great benefits of our partnerships with publishers in other countries was the opportunity to share new ideas and be alert to coming trends. It was essential that in every major publishing territory we cultivated relationships which went deeper than the superficialities of quoting prices and negotiating terms. Market intelligence was what we required on a constant basis, and to this end we sought to hunt in pairs, a senior figure from the creative side or one of the company directors accompanying a sales manager on a trip overseas. The accumulation of such experience was vital to the evaluation of a new topic. For my own part, as publisher, I was in time able to imagine myself in a balloon above the earth, confident enough to make an informed guess at the relative appeal of a proposed book idea in the key territories, and then to have this qualified or endorsed by the senior international sales people with their on-the-ground expertise in a region.

The deeper we could drill down into a market, beyond the publishers to the retailers and special sales outlets, the better. This, of course, applied on a regular basis in our domestic publishing operations, where we sought, and enjoyed, regular presentations and exchanges of ideas with the major customers. It was not unusual, for example, to find all the key category buyers from W.H. Smith assembled round our boardroom table for a show-and-tell session on work in progress followed by a think-tank in which we elicited their feedback on what subject areas were in need of a facelift or a new approach. At one of these discussions a bright spark from their reference section questioned why there had never been a populist history of painting to compete with E.H. Gombrich's perennial *Story of Art* – in other words, a treatment tailored to the average W.H. Smith customer rather than the elite. We agreed to explore the idea. The big question was: who would author such a work?

We gave the project to Sean Moore. He was married to a painter, Patricia Wright, and was the managing editor most in tune with the subject. For a while not much happened. We ran through a catalogue of familiar, or over-familiar, names and found reasons to discard them. Then one day he said to me, 'What about Sister Wendy Beckett?'

'Who?'

'Sister Wendy. She's a Carmelite nun.'

'I've never heard of her.'

'No, but you will. She's going to be on the BBC in the

next few weeks.'

'Talking about art?'

'Yes. And very convincingly. As well as entertainingly. She's a one-off. I've met her.'

'Really? Where?'

'I went to visit her. She lives in a caravan attached to a convent. She's an absolute delight.'

'Did you tell her about this project?'

'Yes, of course. I think she'd be very interested. She would write something original because she responds to pictures in a psychic kind of way. Paintings speak to her. She can extemporise on them straight to camera. The BBC has nicknamed her "One Take Wendy."'

'Well, can you arrange for her to come in and meet us then?'

Sean assured me that could be done on one of her next trips to London to film for the BBC. But he counselled me that Nick Rossiter, the BBC producer who had "discovered" her, had let it slip that Sister Wendy, who lived on bread and water in the solitary seclusion of her caravan, had now awoken to the pleasures of gourmet food and fine wine. After decades of abstinence her virgin palate was untainted and she was determined to enjoy these new sensations of taste and smell to the very limit. I booked a table at the Neal Street Restaurant.

On the appointed day Sister Wendy appeared in the office, a twinkling 60-something with a distinctive toothy grin and a devastating gift for mixing sly cunning with ingenuousness. But her charm was so disabling it was impossible not to be enchanted by her company.

I introduced her to the senior sales and marketing people who were going to join us for lunch. We talked for a few minutes about the book and whether we could create something that could in turn form the basis for a major TV series. Then I asked Sister Wendy if she was ready to go and eat.

'Ooh, yes!' she said, clapping her hands in glee. 'Where are you going to take me?'

I told her that we had booked a table at the most prestigious Italian restaurant in the area.

'Does it have a Michelin star?' enquired Sister Wendy with a wicked glint in her eye.

'I'm not sure. I believe it does. It certainly deserves to have one.'

'My TV pwoducer took me to a place with two stars last night,' she said, poking me in the ribs.

'Oh, right, I can see I'm in the doghouse already,' I said, taking her arm and escorting her downstairs.

Once we were seated in the restaurant Sister Wendy insisted that we choose different dishes from the menu so that we could share the taste of each other's.

'You see,' she explained, 'when I'm in the cawavan at the convent, I live on bwown bwead and water. But when I come to London I like to expewience all the wonderful sensations of tasting new kinds of food. And wine!' she added emphatically. 'Hint, hint!'

Hint, hint, I thought, remembering Karen Black in *Five Easy Pieces*.

'Do you prefer red or white, Sister Wendy?' I enquired.

'Oh, I can dwink a glass or maybe two of wed. But I dwink white by the gallon!' she exclaimed. 'I'm especially fond of Montwachet if by any chance it's on the wine list.'

I scanned the whites. There indeed was a top-of-the-range Montrachet at a cool £80 a bottle. Oh well, I mused, no going back. I'm either going to remember this lunch, or I'm going to be made to forget it. Let's hope she turns out to be a star.

In the event I couldn't remember the lunch at all. Several bottles of Montrachet were easily tucked away by the time we reached the dessert course. The meal was running long, and, soon after, all my colleagues made their excuses and left to catch up with urgent appointments. Then, for me, came the knockout punch.

'Do you know, Chwistopher, I'm exceedingly partial to a particular dessert wine?' said Sister Wendy, clasping my wrist. 'It's called Elysium.'

'Heaven,' I said.

'Yes,' she said, 'but a diffewent kind of heaven. It's here on earth and it's here in this westauwant.'

I am not a man for dessert wines, at least not in quantity and especially not if I have work to do. The Montrachet was already threatening my afternoon's productivity. But as for Sister Wendy, not only did she have the purest palate from her decades of abstinence, she had a head like a mule. The wine seemed to have no effect other than to make her humour more sparkling and her wit more wicked. I wondered uncharitably if 40 years of communion wine had made her immune. After three glasses of Elysium – the third on the house as the proprietor had never seen it consumed in such quantity – I was waving my arms in surrender.

'The bill, the bill. My kingdom for the bill!' I slurred at the waiter.

I was close to the truth. The bill when it came was akin to the GNP of a small African state.

'Dear Chwistopher, have you any idea what time it is?' said Sister Wendy. 'My twain leaves at half past thwee, I think.'

'Well, you can say goodbye to that,' I said, peering woozily at my watch. 'It's already after four.'

'Oh dear, we have been wemiss. Perhaps you could book me into a hotel for tonight? Pwefewably a comfortable one with a minibar in the woom.'

'Five stars?' I enquired. 'Or would four be sufficient? Where does your TV producer put you up? I don't want to find myself always trailing behind his sumptuous coat tails.'

'I like it that you two are competing,' said Sister Wendy with a winning smile. 'It means you both want to attain the highest standards. That way we will have a wonderful TV sewies and a bwilliant book, won't we?'

I borrowed a phone book from the front desk and eventually found an appropriate hotel with availability. I had to provide my credit card details. Another hit. It was already reeling from the lunch bill.

'All sorted,' I said to Sister Wendy. 'Let me get you a taxi.'

'Thank you so much,' she said in her sweetest voice. 'But I haven't any means of paying the taxi.'

'Don't you have any cash on you?' I asked.

'Oh no,' said Sister Wendy, 'I'm not cawwying anything apart fwom my twain ticket and the key to my cawavan.'

I had been to the cashpoint that morning and drawn my maximum daily allowance ahead of the weekend. This wad of notes I now extracted from my back pocket.

'There you are,' I said, swaying unsteadily on the pavement as we waited for a taxi. 'All that I have I give unto thee.'

'Now, Chwistopher, you mustn't take the words of Our Lord in vain.'

'I'm not. It's true. Believe me, Sister Wendy, you are welcome to it. We are going to make the most exquisite book ever published in the annals of art history, and you are going to be the brightest star in the firmament. This, as the man said at the end of *Casablanca*, is the beginning of a beautiful friendship.'

'What's *Casablanca*?' said Sister Wendy.

But just then a taxi drew up.

'It's a love story,' I said as I helped her into the cab. It had started to rain.

'Oh, you're a twue womantic!' squealed Sister Wendy, waving to me as the taxi sped off. Her toothy grin filled the rear window like a Muppet.

My God, I thought, as I leaned against a lamppost with the rain hammering on my wine-sozzled head. I've been clobbered. I'm broke. I'm soaked to the skin. And, would you believe it, for the first time in my life, I've been drunk under the table. By a nun!

Inevitably the compilation of Sister Wendy's book, *The Story of Painting*, was never less than interesting – as everyone who came into contact with her can attest, as they were alternately charmed and manipulated into giving her what she wanted. Sean and Patricia (who acted as her amanuensis) did a wonderful job escorting Sister Wendy to various galleries and museums, including trips across the Atlantic. On one of the latter, Sister Wendy caused some consternation among the security staff at Heathrow when she set off the alarm as she went through the arch. The pockets of a nun's habit are evidently remarkably deep, as the increasingly incredulous expressions of the security personnel testified when Sister Wendy began emptying hers. Eventually, an impressive array of miscellaneous objects – including keys, spectacles, coins, a corkscrew and a selection of miniatures – was ranged across the counter top. I think security may have briefly wondered if her nun's habit was a disguise, but someone had seen her on television, and soon they were asking for her autograph.

The Story of Painting was a hit, especially in the US. Here in the UK her TV series was predictably derided by the up-their-own-arse art critics, but in America she was embraced without cynicism. I took her to dinner to celebrate, failed to get a table at Bibendum (another favourite of hers) and was once again deemed to have come up short in comparison to her TV producer. Over a bottle of Montrachet (natch) we talked about what she might write next. And then, as the wine loosened my tongue, I mentioned that Linda and I were thinking of going on a long weekend to Paris to celebrate our silver wedding. It suddenly occurred to me what fun it would be if Sister Wendy came too – she could give us a guided tour of her favourite pictures in the Louvre and the Musée d'Orsay, and we could take her to eat at some fabulous restaurants. It seemed like the best idea in the world just then, and she thought so too. As we left the restaurant, she asked me if I could do her a small favour.

'Sure. What is it?'

'Well, you know the hotel the BBC puts me in in Kensington. I weally don't like their house white wine. I have asked for a fwidge to be put in my woom, so I can buy my own wine to keep cool. But I now have to be there all this weekend and I haven't had time to buy any. Do you think we could find some now?'

I looked at my watch. It was around 10.30. The off-licences were closing.

'I'll try,' I said, 'but we may be too late.'

So it came to pass that I found myself driving Sister Wendy around the streets of Kensington in search of a bottle. I spotted one off-licence whose lights were still on, but the doors were locked. A woman was counting the takings at the till. I banged on the window. She looked up. I pointed to my car and mimed with as much urgency as I could muster. She stared at me as though I was a lunatic, then switched off the light. I climbed back into the car.

'Sorry, Sister Wendy, she wouldn't respond to my pleading.'

'Never mind,' she replied. 'But I did love your body language.'

I'm turning into a circus clown, I thought. We drove west along Kensington High Street. I saw another glimmer of lights in an off-licence. No luck. I walked back towards the car. Two Irishmen were standing close to it.

'Excuse me, mister,' one of them said. 'Is that the beloved Sister Wendy you have in there by any chance? We'd love to say hello to her, and maybe ask for a little blessing.'

'Tell you what,' I said. 'I'll let you say hello to her if you can tell me where I can buy a decent bottle of white wine at this time of night.'

'Sure,' the other replied. 'There's a corner shop that stays open late in a little street just opposite Olympia. He has a bottle or two.'

A few minutes later, with some disquiet, I parked my Merc in a sinister little alley near the corner shop. Inside, to my surprise and relief, I discovered some relatively decent white wines on display. I returned to the car clutching the blue and white plastic bag in which three bottles were clinking.

'Success!' I exclaimed.

'Bwavo!' said Sister Wendy, clapping her hands like a child.

'So do you have a corkscrew or do I need to go back and buy one?'

'Dear Chwistopher, on my twavels I may occasionally forget my nightdwess, but I never forget my corkscwew!'

Nobody's going to believe this, I thought. Here I am at eleven o'clock at night, in my car in an unlit cul-de-sac with a nun and three bottles of wine (not Three Nuns, I hasten to add)… I need to deliver her back to her hotel.

As we approached the front entrance, Sister Wendy exclaimed at the sight of the doorman.

'There's dear John!' she cried, climbing out of the car to

greet him.

'John,' she said, as I moved round the car to say goodbye, 'this is my publisher, Chwistopher. He and his wife are going to take me to Pawis for a weekend. Would you like to come too?'

The next day I repeated this story to people in the office.

'Oh,' they all said, 'what a great idea! Can we come as well?'

Suddenly it looked as though I would have to block book Eurostar as all our colleagues clamoured to follow Sister Wendy, the Pied Piper of food, wine and art, to Paris.

Alas, it didn't happen, not even on a modest scale. Sister Wendy became temporarily unwell and was advised to avoid travelling for a time. What might have been an unforgettable experience became a lost weekend, so I never had the chance to raise my glass to her and say 'We'll always have Paris'. But then she hadn't ever seen *Casablanca*…

 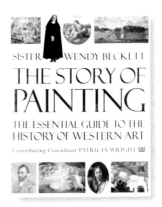

Sister Wendy achieved celebrity status, especially in the USA, where her TV series and appearances on late night chat shows charmed and amused the general public.

Gandhi in Las Vegas

The following year, 1995, Bill Gates sold his stake in Dorling Kindersley, garnering what to most people would be counted as a handsome profit on his investment but was merely pocket money to him. Doubtless he could see that DK wasn't going to drive Microsoft to new stratospheric levels and our strategic value to him was strictly limited. For those of us on the DK board it was something of a relief to be independent again. The Microsoft relationship had been beneficial in that it had forced us to raise our game as a company, but from the outset we operated in different hemispheres from each other, both financially and culturally, and the gap was never likely to be bridged.

Microsoft's exit forced us into a rethink about the strategic future of DK. Although the partnership with Gates and the subsequent public flotation had generated funding, the engine room of the company's growth over the past twenty years had been fuelled entirely organically. We were now persuaded that the dramatic upward curve of the last seven years (£10 million – £139 million) couldn't be sustained indefinitely. Our international sales people were starting to reach the outer limits of the known world, there was more competition in the marketplace, and imitators churned out look-alike versions of our children's books. While there was as yet no real evidence of global saturation, we knew that it was essential to plan beyond the immediate future. In the short term it was argued that even if the books business stalled, any decline in revenues could be more than compensated by the imminent lift-off of either Multimedia or DKFL or, in Peter Kindersley's opinion, both. DK's future as a player in the digital world and as a force for good in the area of home education was now what principally occupied his working hours. He was even recorded as saying around this time, in a quote that repeatedly came back to haunt him, that 'the book is dead'. He subsequently denied the remark, but whether or not he actually said it, it accurately captured the way his vision for the future was being mapped in his own mind.

There was another, as yet unexploited, option for growth: acquisition. One of our long-term competitors, Quarto, appeared to have generated much of its growth from the gradual accumulation of a raft of small companies. At DK, during the 1990s, we spent a proportion of our time on the lookout for businesses that might be a good fit. There were various companies or lists that became available and attracted our attention, but the fit was always the problem. The DK design style was now distinctive enough and pervasive enough to be acknowledged as our defining hallmark. Thus any acquisition would either have to be restyled to blend in with the company image or be so distinctly different as to be recognised as a discrete business.

As it happened, the first acquisition we did succeed in completing was a hybrid of the two. Henderson Publishing was in bad shape; it had traded successfully for several years on the back of its popular *Funfax* series, but this was now running out of steam. The notion behind DK's decision to buy the company was to gain access to the children's "self-purchase" market. It was a mistake. There was a world of difference between the quality, mass-market children's information books that DK was producing and the deliberately cheap and cheerful Funfax offerings.

The deal might have made more sense, though not much, if we had been willing to run it as an entirely separate business. But that was not the Kindersley way. Anything he owned he had to tinker with, and as far as Henderson was concerned, that meant trying to inject its titles with some of the DK design values – about as fruitless an ambition as training a mule for the Derby. Barry Henderson understood the market he was serving and he delivered what it wanted, just as DK understood its market and provided for it. There were no editors or designers within DK who knew how to produce a book for the racks in Woolworths; their training was to beautify, to embroider, to offer aesthetic purity on the page. What was required here was, in design terms, closer to a comic book style, preferably laced with cartoonish artwork and cracker-style jokes. And there was no enthusiasm for the deal from any of the sales people, particularly in the US where we consistently failed to get *Funfax* titles any exposure at all in the retail market. It was an unhappy five-year marriage, and the only beneficiary was Barry Henderson himself, who was ultimately able to restart his business under a new name, rehire the staff we had laid off, and reoccupy his former premises in Woodbridge as though the DK episode had never happened.

The Henderson acquisition was a small, if irritating, distraction. It was never going to deliver the extra chunk of sales which might prove transformational to our figures. Within DK, however, Multimedia was starting to motor; in its first year of publishing it generated £13 million in turnover, with over 300,000 English language copies sold of its first five titles, led by the best-selling *The Way Things Work*. DKFL was also burgeoning – in the UK it had won the New Business Award from the Direct Selling Association and was now contributing to profits. The focus of management attention had now switched to the US, where the distributor numbers had tripled but were still only pinpricks on the face of that vast continent. This was the real breeding ground for Peter Kindersley's new religion.

Missionary zeal was certainly the phrase that came to mind when attending a DKFL annual conference. These events were as far removed from the normal realms of publishing activity as one could imagine. Unlike a regular trade sales conference, the products were secondary. The primary agenda was indoctrination and the rebirth of faith – faith in themselves, in their business, in the company, and in the power to achieve amazing goals that would in turn deliver for them all that they desired in life: wealth, independence, job satisfaction, and the respect of their peers. These sales conferences took place in a different city each year and all followed more or less the same pattern. One in Las Vegas stands out in my memory.

I sat next to Peter on the flight from London. While I dozed in front of some crappy movie, he was buried in the autobiography of Gandhi. He was extracting quotations and adding them to his speech notes for the conference. Every so often he would grip my elbow.

'Listen to this, Christo. It's really interesting what Gandhi says here.'

This is going to be a first, I thought, a captain of industry in the capital of Mammon invoking the wisdom of Gandhi. If I make one bet in Las Vegas, it would be odds-on that this has never happened before.

The conference attendees were lodged in a scrofulous $64 day-for-night hotel where the blinds in the rooms were permanently drawn. On every floor, in every available space, in the bar, on the breakfast counter, in the lobby, the legions of slot machines were ranged. Before them sat the punters, catatonically pulling and releasing the handle with that dead look in their eyes, feeding in coins, pulling and releasing… Occasionally the low hum that permeated the hotel was punctuated by a cascade of small coins dropping into the tray, and one of the robotic figures would briefly come to life, punch the air and fill his cup.

'Yeah, man, yeah. You beauty, you baby.'

I couldn't imagine a place less conducive to the promotion of books and the exchange of ideas. But Alan Luce had justified the choice on the grounds that the distributors had to pay for their own travel and accommodation, and Las Vegas offered cheap flights and cheap hotels if you avoided the glitzy emporia.

Once they were all seated within the conference room, however, the distractions were eliminated. There were indeed more than a thousand of them, eager, bright eyed, a newly minted DKFL catalogue clasped like a winning lottery ticket in their fervid paws, awaiting the descent of Peter Kindersley from Olympus. As the lights dimmed, the babble in the hall quietened to a low hum of expectation. In the background the reedy whispers of Crosby, Stills, Nash & Young exhorted them to teach their children well, while images of happy offspring playing, reading, watching, listening, jumping and running spooled across the stage curtain.

A clash of cymbals, an unctuous roll of drums. Then, from the speaker system, the fruitily melodramatic tones of an underachieving amateur thesp: 'Ladies and gentlemen, would you please now put your hands together and give a very warm welcome to the Founder, Chairman and Chief Executive of Dorling Kindersley, our uniquely inspired and inspiring leader, the one and only Peter Kindersley!'

The curtains parted, the disciples rose as one, lifting their applauding hands above their heads to salute the chief magician in their theatre of dreams. And there, in the spotlight centre stage, stood the slightly diffident figure of Peter, bowing and waving to the multitude, acknowledging the cheers and whistles with his not entirely self-deprecating smile.

Once the ovations and the cat calls had subsided, and he was there in the fierce glow of the arc lights, milking the moment before launching into his oration, this was the point at which I, from my watching position in the wings, wondered whether the wheel of the company had turned. This is no longer a business, I reflected, it is now a religion. Peter may seduce them with his carefully modulated speech laced with spiritual nuggets from Gandhi's philosophy of life, but is he at the same moment separating himself from the collective of the group and confirming his status as The One and Only? Hubris and humility make poor bedfellows, I mused, as he finished speaking and the audience clambered over the seats to claim his attention, relate their personal stories, ask for reassurance or guidance, and touch, if they were lucky, some tiny fibre of his garment. There was no doubt that this was a highly effective means of ratcheting up the growth of DKFL. The word would spread and people would flock from all corners of the continent. But I knew, even as I thought it, that the character of DK as a whole could be altered from now on and the dynamics of the company shifted.

After a break for coffee, the meeting reconvened to hear the exhortations from the leading distributors of DKFL. It was a strange cocktail of penitence and triumphalism. Somebody would be summoned to the podium to recount her rags-to-riches life story – how she had been a single mother living in some godforsaken tenement with no visible means of support when she had been introduced to someone working as a distributor for DKFL, how she had been recruited and her life transformed. Now, weeping occasionally with emotion and simultaneously cheered by the audience as she told her story, she was living with her daughter in a swanky condo by the sea, had been able to move her mother into a place nearby, was driving a new car and taking a cruise vacation to the Caribbean this coming year.

'So, folks!' she shouted, punching the air, 'that's what you can achieve through the power of DKFL. That's why we all have to go onward and upward and never, ever give up.

Because the Lord has brought Peter Kindersley to us with all his wonderful books and you can go out there and save the lives of others just as my life was saved.'

By now the distributors were on their feet, weeping, laughing, cheering, hugging each other. After several of these powerful testimonials they were all wrung out with emotion. It was time to skewer them with the business end of the meeting.

Alan Luce, a master at speaking without notes, patrolled the stage with the microphone, unfurling his labyrinthine sentences and listening to the echo as his portentous declarations reverberated back to him.

'You gotta walk the walk and talk the talk!' he intoned. 'And then you've gotta walk the talk. You folks know what I mean?'

I guess they did. I hadn't a clue. It sounded like scaffolding falling into a bath. Fifteen minutes later Alan sat down and Peter Cartwright took up the baton. While his approach was less earnest than Alan's, and his speech sprinkled with groan-making jokes ('He must have kept the insides of every cracker he's ever pulled,' somebody whispered to me), he wandered off into a lengthy anecdote about his childhood, which focused on his mother's entreaties to 'eat your greens'. There was a message in there somewhere. But the nub of both Alan and Peter's addresses was to rack up the recruitment of new distributors and drive up the volume of sales.

The last session was devoted to the presentation of new titles. As I stood in the spotlight on the stage facing a thousand pairs of eyes in the darkened room, I too felt the surge of messianic power, an audience that loved what we were delivering to them, lives that were in our gift to transform. I expect Linda also felt it when she addressed them, and Roger Priddy too. Roger was the highly gifted creative director of children's books for the younger age groups, and therefore responsible for many of DKFL's best-selling titles. As he was both amusing and good looking, the distributors always looked forward to his presentations with giddy expectation.

Afterwards, as we mingled in the throng, we witnessed close up the effect our books were having. Linda, whose job was increasingly focused on creating exclusive product for the DKFL businesses, had invented an engaging character called P.B. Bear around whom several books and even a CD-ROM had been published. And, best of all, P.B. Bear was now available to them as a charming plush toy. The distributors were ecstatic. As she walked among them, a woman tearfully grabbed her arm.

'Linda, you saved my life. My little boy wouldn't accept any soft toys until you brought us P.B. Bear. And now, thanks to him, little Brett has learned to read as well.'

Bear

It was impossible not to be moved by the visible effect we could have on the fortunes of others, especially those from a disadvantaged background who were desperate to climb up from it on the ladder that education could provide. But Linda, Roger and I were only supporting acts to the Kindersley starring role. I was concerned about the potentially damaging effects on him from continued exposure to such excessive adulation.

We flew back to London. At dawn we climbed into my car in the Heathrow long-term car park.

'Peter,' I said as I turned the key in the ignition, 'you know, you've got to be careful about this DKFL worship. You might start to believe it…'

He grabbed my hand as it rested on the gear stick.

'Christo, thank you for saying that. I know it is a risk. But if I ever forget, if I do start to behave as though I believe it, promise me you'll tell me. You will, won't you?'

He looked me straight in the eye. He meant it. I wouldn't forget.

95 Madison Avenue

The fabulous bull run of Dorling Kindersley's organically expanding universe effectively peaked after eight years, in 1996. It was certainly the last year when growth came easily to us, when it didn't require hoisting by artificial means, by cutting and scrimping and saving and hustling down other avenues to bolster the sales. It was the last of the best of times. We were still having fun.

Nowhere was this more true than in the US. Under John Sargent's shrewd and inspiring leadership, the offices of DK Inc, now at 95 Madison Avenue in New York, were buzzing. A satellite operation can be hard to maintain, particularly when it is not autonomous, when the company ethos and the core products originate in the mother ship on another continent. But even though their day-to-day labours were mainly focused on Americanising and adapting what we created in London, the staff at DK Inc were uniformly supportive of what the company was aiming to achieve, and believed, as we did, that the pride they took in their work would find its reward in the books' positive embrace by the American public. And the marketing and publicity departments, led by Chuck Lang and Allison Devlin, were stretching every creative sinew to ensure that our books were out there and highly visible.

As a result, DK Inc enjoyed some remarkable local successes. The North American edition of *The Birdfeeder Handbook*, 98 per cent changed from the European edition we had published in the UK and now branded with the imprimatur of the Audubon Society, sold more than 250,000 copies. Likewise a partnership with the American Horticultural Society to rework our RHS gardening encyclopedias for the US market brought us branded authority for this backlist category. And a symbiotic relationship had been developed with the Smithsonian Institution over a range of reference titles; over a decade we produced more than 50 titles in association with them, to the benefit of both parties, until a new marketing broom in Washington decided to make his mark by negotiating an exclusive block deal with Harper Collins. This resulted in over-publishing and may have damaged the aura of the Smithsonian's authority.

After five years of publishing in the US, our name was established and the brand well recognised. Well, to be accurate, the name – Dorling Kindersley – wasn't easily lodged in the American memory. It had too many soft consonants to trip easily off the tongue.

'Oh, I love your faggy English names!' exclaimed an effete Anglophile bookseller as he stood in front of our booth at ABA. But that was a minority view. The Yanks just couldn't get their heads around the pronunciation or the spelling, and soon the notice board in the kitchen area of the office was festooned with variations clipped from incoming mail – from Darling Kiddley to Dorking Kindly and, best of all, Drooling Kinderfly. DK, on the other hand, the logo and the shorthand for the imprint, was a shoe-in and its eventual adoption over there, against the wishes of Peter Kindersley, who didn't appreciate the linguistic nuances, was thankfully sealed.

While our distinctive style of cut-out photography on white backgrounds (with the drop shadow) was no longer a novelty – and in the UK was increasingly mimicked by cheaper competitors – it still struck a strong chord with the great American public. First print runs of new lead titles for that market were regularly in the 35,000–50,000 copies bracket and would sell through in a matter of months. We reached a point, after just five years as an imprint in the US, where our sales outstripped those of Houghton Mifflin's trade division, which was repping the list. The HM sales force had done a good job – no doubt they enjoyed the leverage which some of DK's sexier titles gave them to persuade buyers to up the ante on the more arcane volumes in their own catalogue – and the management had been generous in granting DK as much time as we needed to promote our wares at their sales conferences. Joe Kanon was unfailingly supportive, but he must have known that we would seek to fly with our own wings once the numbers were there to justify the hiring of our own sales team. It says a lot for his sense of decency, as well as the friendship he and John Sargent had forged, that he allowed us to extricate ourselves in a civilised manner that left no hard feelings on either side.

That, however, marked the end of an era. Soon after, Joe Kanon left the gamekeeping side of the publishing business to turn author, and was rewarded with a bestseller on his first attempt. He submitted *Los Alamos* anonymously, but a canny editor who knew him guessed the identity of the author from one of his familiar catchphrases – 'No good deed goes unpunished'. As far as I can tell, this maxim hasn't impeded his writing career as he continues to produce successful intricately plotted fiction set against various backgrounds in the aftermath of World War II.

Then, for DK, in July 1996 came the hammer blow. John Sargent left to take over from Tom McCormack at St Martin's Press and head up the Holtzbrinck operation in the US. Just as it was inevitable that DK would outgrow Houghton Mifflin, so it was that John would sooner or later be snapped up by bigger fish. For us, the sooner part was the problem. Later, much later, would have been our wish. But there was nothing we could do, and our pockets were way too shallow to match the packages that the heavy hitters could offer without blinking. He subsequently told me that at least two other big players had previously tried to tempt him away with a more or less carte blanche offer to write his own cheque. So, in retrospect, we were fortunate to keep him for the time he stayed. But his departure left a gaping hole, both in the management of the US business and in its collective personality, and the staff, especially the senior members who worked closely with him, were absolutely bereft.

Not only was John difficult to replace in person, the job

itself proved tough to fill. It didn't carry enough prestige or independence to attract candidates already well-established in the business; the ideal person would be, like John Sargent, a rising star who, while likely viewing the job as an interim platform from which to launch a career upwards, would be determined to make a mark and would therefore throw all his or her energy into driving the business forward. The role also required a personal skill set that enabled positive rapprochement with the London management, especially Peter Kindersley, and the confidence to prove to him that you were capable of taking bold initiatives while at the same time not going against the grain of the Supreme Will. And the position did not come with fancy executive trappings – big office, big desk, acres of carpet for underlings to cross in deferential submission, business class travel, etc. Instead there was an average-sized desk inside a transparent glass box in a corner of a large open-plan floor, a goldfish bowl into which everyone could, and did, peer, and it was shared with two other senior execs. Transatlantic flights were cattle class. It was no place for the self-important.

The person we did hire, Kristina Petersen, was not in the least self-important, but the lack of privacy was a real problem for her. It seems that within a week of joining DK she had realised that she had made a mistake, that the company style was so far removed from her previous experience with Random House and she couldn't find a way to bridge the gap. She never felt comfortable, and left after a year. A shame – in different circumstances she might have flourished.

Once again we had to go back to the well. But the bucket

came up empty, and for six months the role of CEO of DK Inc was vacant, a completely unsatisfactory state of affairs in the company's biggest market. Rod Hare, Group MD, and David Holmes, who became Group Sales and Marketing Director in 1997, made regular commutes to New York to patch the hole, but this was no substitute for on-the-ground leadership, and the US operation wobbled uncertainly until Danny Gurr crossed the floor from retailing – he had been CEO of Lauriat's Books – to occupy the empty seat in the spring of 1998.

There were other distractions in the aftermath of John Sargent's departure. Before he left he had had an informal discussion in the elevator of 95 Madison Avenue with Neal Porter, then with Orchard Books on another floor of the building. This had been prompted by the notion that DK, now recognised in the US as the market leader in quality non-fiction for kids, could become more complete as a children's publisher if it also delivered fiction and picture books, and coincided with the whispers on the wind that Neal and two of his colleagues, Richard Jackson and Melanie Kroupa, were deeply disaffected at Orchard and looking for an exit. When they decided to migrate to DK Inc, it aroused the wrath of Arnaud Lagardère, the supremo of Hachette, which owned Orchard, who instigated legal proceedings that rumbled on for about a year. These took up a huge amount of management time and expense, especially on the part of Anita Fulton, the DK legal director, who had to spend weeks across the Atlantic to battle the case through. Eventually it was settled out of court.

The advent of the new "author-led" children's list in the US had a mixed reception. Many of the staff were ecstatic; they saw it as an opportunity to create and market "their" books – in other words, US-originated titles as opposed to the constant stream of UK books that, like them or not, they were obliged to adapt and promote. On the other hand, just as with the children's illustrated fiction list that Linda was building in the UK, the signals from the sales force were confused. It was one thing to create *Eyewitness Classics*, well-known children's stories retold and handsomely illustrated, because with their sidebars of factual information, showing details of contemporary life, they looked like DK books. Whether there was really a market for them and whether readers liked having the narrative interrupted by such diversions was another matter. But to build a full-scale traditional children's list, such as Neal and his cohorts were doing, was equivalent to saying to the reps that DK was going to be like any other publisher, and they were puzzled by the lack of clear demarcation lines. In fact, everyone, including those responsible for creating the list, was to varying degrees mystified. The addition of a whole new programme of novels and picture books at the tail end of a trade sales conference always seemed like an uncomfortable afterthought, no matter how worthy or appealing the books. One might say that, like the acquisition of Funfax, the corporate imperatives of growth had led us for a second time to ignore the cardinal rule of sticking to the knitting.

It didn't help that there was never a true meeting of the minds between the DKFL operations and the trade businesses. Bizarrely, in the US, this manifested itself as a class war, between the perceived elitism of the Manhattanites and the folksy evangelism of the Orlando group. However much each side protested, and they did protest too much, and for all the urgings from London management to work together as one to capitalise on building the DK brand in the great republic, they resolutely refused to blend, to share marketing initiatives, to cooperate at even the most basic level. If it did occasionally happen, it seemed to be with much gritting of teeth, and if it didn't work out, there were sly asides about mendacity and mistrust. It usually came to a head in a group gathering where Peter was present. Some of the DKFL executives were particularly adept at publicly pronouncing what he wanted to hear and then contravening it in practice. Everyone had their own agenda.

There was one title, however, on which all parties were agreed and which made a significant difference to the 1996 year-end results. *Children Just Like Me* was a Kindersley family project, conceived by Peter and executed by Barnabas, his photographer son, and Anabel, his daughter-in-law. It was produced in collaboration with UNICEF and consisted of profiles of the daily life of children all round the world – where they lived, what they ate, where they went to school, how they played… It was a classic DK compilation, vivid, graphic, eye-opening and instantly appealing, and it received the marketing it merited. Published in the autumn of 1995, it sold over 350,000 copies in 23 markets in its first nine months, and the smiling image of the young girl waving on the front cover became one of the company's defining images.

Thus, when we presented the results in September 1996,

we could proudly demonstrate a business firing on all cylinders – turnover up 26 per cent to £174 million with pre-tax profits of £13 million. The US had grown by 40 per cent in the year, and had doubled in two years. DKFL was up by 76 per cent, and Multimedia by 62 per cent, the latter now over £21 million in spite of the downward pressure on retail prices, especially in the US. DK Direct and DK Vision also recorded uplifts in revenues, while DK Adult and DK Children's could point to successful frontlist publishing backed by the powerhouses of their backlists. We had managed to negotiate the choppy discounting waters stirred up by the demise of the Net Book Agreement without a significant loss of margin. In total, some 40 million DK books were sold during the year. Boom time.

A book that encapsulated the best qualities of DK – original, attractive, accessible, informative, and universally appealing.

Complexity and Commitment

It may sound like a recipe for chaos but Dorling Kindersley thrived on complexity, both creatively and operationally.

In the first instance, the designs on the page, in particular those with the *Eyewitness* look, are deliberately complex. They may appear open and simple to use by the reader – and that was the ultimate goal – but hidden within them are layers of built-in hierarchy to provide special emphasis or establish points of difference. The relative sizes of the images and how they are placed on the spread, the different sizes of font, the use of annotation, the positioning of captions adjacent to an image, are all worked out to a template with the aim of, firstly, creating an emotional impact with which to draw in the reader, and, secondly, allowing that reader to graze the page and, like snaffling canapés at a drinks party, ingest bite-sized chunks of information. Nothing too heavy, but cumulatively satisfying.

Those who dismissed the *Eyewitness Guides* as being all pictures and not enough substance hadn't looked closely enough. In its 64 pages an *Eyewitness* contains approximately 15,000 words. It is the manner in which the text is scattered around the page that is deceptive. And yet so beneficial to the reluctant reader who would shrivel up at the prospect of 15,000 words presented, page after page, in solid walls of type. But here, spread across the tablecloth of the white background like a tempting buffet of morsels – and I have witnessed this with such readers – the prospect of absorbing the words is no longer daunting but positively to be enjoyed.

The crucial element is the proximity of the text to the image it describes. This style of design came to be known as Lexigraphics, and Peter Kindersley would give interviews and deliver lectures about the art and science of Words and Pictures whenever an opportunity presented itself. He took his inspiration from the Swedish design guru, Sven Lidman, whose mantra was, "Through the picture I see reality, through the word I understand it". The core of Peter's message was that pictures are fast to absorb, and words are slow, but if they are placed side-by-side, the effect is to equalise the speed of their impact – the image speeds up the words, and the words slow down the image. It sounded convincing. The way in which we had originally arrived at the *Eyewitness* style of design may have had more to do with art than science, but now he could bolster its worldwide success with the plausible notion that it was proving its worth as an effective learning tool, one that would be the key instrument in DK's ultimate drive to be an educational publisher.

We launched our first US publishing list with an ad campaign headed "What Is A Fish?" It began with a picture of a carp, and no text; this was succeeded by a description of a carp, and no image; the clinching spread that followed was an *Eyewitness* treatment of a carp with varying levels of text, captions and annotation surrounding the same image of the fish, utterly transformed and made both more interesting and more dramatic by its juxtaposition of words and pictures.

This neat advertising campaign offered an effective eye-opener into the complexities and subtle benefits of the Eyewitness page design.

This artful complexity was at the heart of DK's success at maintaining its pole position as the premier producer of illustrated non-fiction for so many years. Others might imitate, but usually cut corners and short-changed the buyer of their books with more superficial treatments of a topic. It also explained why DK books were so costly to originate – the editors and designers were schooled in this exacting style, and such was the desire for perfectionism instilled in them by their leader that the proofs of a title were subject to endless fiddling, improving and correcting, even of the tiniest details, while the typesetting and reproduction costs rose ever higher. Ultimately, some editors and designers were so rigidly indoctrinated that they couldn't release themselves from the "fiddle factor", and outsourcers producing work for them found it an impossible task to get sign-off on their submissions.

The advantage to the foreign language customers of *Eyewitness* books was that they were buying in a unique product, something that they could not have created themselves. But in generating pages that would prove feasible to translate, the DK designers had to be mindful of the space they allowed for those foreign languages that habitually run longer than English. This, along with avoiding items of nationalist, ethnic or class bias on a page, was all part of the complexity of producing illustrated content for a global readership.

As the company grew, so the challenge of satisfying this readership increased, particularly where the choice of titles was concerned. To be both a publisher and a packager is a strangely schizophrenic existence as the demands of one do not necessarily coincide with the needs of the other. As our publishing lists expanded in the US and the UK, and usually generated more revenue per title than could be achieved by the sale of foreign language co-editions, so the balance of the programme tended to shift in favour of the English language markets. There was a period when it went too far and we erroneously neglected the needs of international sales. This partly stemmed from the perpetual demands for growth.

In the US, particularly under the stewardship of Danny Gurr, it was reckoned that the number of reference titles we could produce in any given year for the global market would be insufficient to sustain the necessary upward curve in sales volume. It was therefore deemed necessary to add titles of local interest to boost the numbers – in due course Sean Moore from the Adult division and Andrew Berkhut from Children's were seconded to the US office to generate a list for DK Inc that would retain the DK production values but would generate sufficient sales in that market to cover the origination costs. Thus we created titles on the Civil War, on the Presidents, on the national passions for baseball, football, wrestling and stock car racing, and so forth.

The general imbalance was later exacerbated by the conclusions of a management consultancy exercise that had recommended the establishment of category publishers within the creative divisions. The thinking was sound enough – we had powerful backlists in pregnancy, childcare, gardening, medical reference, travel, children's reference and pre-school. The specific challenge was to capitalise on those strengths and "own" the category in the bookshop ahead of all our competitors. This wasn't a problem with children's books as we were already the major player in the non-fiction sector, both domestically and internationally, and almost all the titles found a ready market around the world. With adult books it was different. In the initial division of the subject areas, Jackie Douglas became category publisher for medical, David Lamb for gardening, pet care and wine, Daphne Razazan for health and cookery. They focused their minds on how to expand their franchises. But then it came to the point when we held our regular forum for brainstorming new ideas ahead of an upcoming book fair, a meeting at which all the markets were represented and I, as group publisher, tended to occupy the role of referee.

'I think there's room for another yoga book,' said Daphne. 'In a smaller format than our existing yoga titles.'

The US and UK welcomed the idea – yoga was still a popular topic – but the international markets questioned whether Norway or Denmark, for example, could absorb another book on the subject.

David proposed a new dog training guide, again welcomed by the English language markets, but only marginally supported by the co-edition sales force.

'Poland only needs one dog training book,' said Antony Melville.

Jackie suggested a title on childhood obesity, but again this was not yet of relevance to the Mediterranean markets.

Danny Gurr, as in many of these meetings, wanted a book on guns for the American hunting fraternity.

'I can sell 30,000 straight off,' he said.

But nobody else bought the idea, and although we might have made a modest profit on such a book on the US sales, I vetoed it on the grounds that I was not interested in going down the road of promotional publishing for rednecks.

This complex balancing act between the publishing and packaging arms was a typical scenario, and as time went on, the divisions between the markets tended to widen rather than diminish. We were becoming a victim of our own success, and there was a danger that in the rush to please the City analysts, we would move further away from our core strengths and closer to becoming just A.N. Other Publisher.

If achieving consensus on the publishing programme was a complicated exercise, delivering it was a pretty formidable challenge. It doesn't take much imagination to grasp that supplying 40 million books in multiple formats in multiple languages to multiple destinations is anything but simple. The unsung heroes of DK's expansion were the production department and the fulfilment department. The plain truth was that life got harder for them every year – more new titles, more revised editions, more markets, more languages, more formats (until we were forced to rationalise them) – and, as the pressures on the creative side increased, more schedules running late. "I love to hear the whoosh of a deadline rushing by," as Douglas Adams famously said. Well, it was not a sentiment shared by Lorraine Baird or Martyn Longly who successively, and very successfully, ran the production department in those expanding years. Martyn was perhaps fortunate in that he didn't have much hair to tear out, and it was no surprise to his friends that when he eventually decided to leave the DK sweatshop he opted for the less frenetic rhythms of life on a West Country farm.

As for the fulfilment department, every day in the cramped space they occupied seemed like Christmas Eve in the post office. Not only were they supplying copies of sample sales materials – sales documents, spreads, dummy jackets – to every potential customer around the world, they were mailing proofs, texts, positioning guides and schedules to those who had contracted to acquire a title and were now translating. The number of pages they handled in a year ran into the hundreds of thousands. We were lucky that the person in charge of this maelstrom of activity, Chris Braham, was actually the calmest person on the planet – outwardly at least. After moving from books to handle the fulfilment and foreign

One wall of DK's fortress-like Frankfurt stand, whose impenetrable structure provoked complaints of paranoia and exclusivity from those not admitted except by appointment.

language conversions of CD-ROMs – possibly an even more demanding assignment – she left for the comparatively Zen-like peace of a life in Japan.

And then there was the week-in week-out complexity behind the organisation of sales trips by the international contingent, and the management of the massive DK army that invaded the book fairs – Frankfurt, Bologna, London, and to a lesser extent, ABA (now BEA). At the height of DK's selling activity, there were more than 30 tables on the stand at Frankfurt, each one dedicated to a separate market or group of territories, all fully occupied on the peak days from dawn to dusk with perhaps as many as 1,500 meetings taking place over the course of the fair. Every year it was a familiar refrain from publishers, agents, authors and others that the DK stand was a fortress to which it was impossible to gain access. They were offended, and we were accused of arrogance. But the simple fact was that there wasn't actually room on the booth for casual visitors. Perhaps we were a little robust in our refusal to grant entry without an appointment. The chief rottweiler on the gate – and also the foreign sales department's chief organiser of fair bookings, hotels, transport, and management of the diary – was the formidable Peggy King.

'Have you got an appointment?' she would demand of anyone who dared to transgress her hallowed space.

'No, but I would like to – '

'I'm sorry, you can't come in without an appointment,' she would interject, barring the way through with her sturdy frame and propelling the visitor firmly back toward the aisle.

Occasionally this resulted in some embarrassing fall-out.

There are senior people in the global publishing village who have no need – and almost certainly no desire – to wear the identifying badge. One such is Florian Langenscheidt, perhaps the most elegant man in German publishing and, as a member of a great publishing dynasty, a Very Important Customer. DK Multimedia were at an advanced stage of persuading him to invest in their programme of CD-ROMs by acquiring the German language rights. So it was a decidedly tricky moment when we discovered that he had received the Peggy treatment and been frogmarched off the stand. Fortunately, Paget Hetherington, who had been negotiating with Florian, was able, with her calculating amalgam of flirtatious charm and faux naivety, to win him round.

Peggy, it has to be said, is a really good sort and she did a really good job. She was also PA to Ruth Sandys, in the latter's capacity as international sales director and then as MD of Children's. Among Peggy's functions were all kinds of tasks relating, it seemed, more to the running of Ruth's life than the management of a publishing division. One of these was to ensure that she was continuously supplied with chocolate in one form or another. Every Friday afternoon, when I had a weekly catch-up with Ruth in her office, I would get a call from Peggy beforehand.

'Hello, Christopher, she would love it if you would bring her a tub of that double Belgian chocolate ice cream.' Or some such.

I would cross Henrietta Street to the newsagent and scrabble around in the freezer in search of the treat of the day. Then I would cut through St Paul's Churchyard to King Street, carrying my trophy. By four o'clock on a Friday afternoon the churchyard was usually well-populated with the local winos. On one occasion, I was strolling past them holding a gigantic chocolate and vanilla confection in a cornet when I was assailed by a staggering Scotsman.

'Oi, Pavarotti!' he slurred as he swayed in my path, 'Gi' us a song!'

'See the gauntlet I have to run, Peggy,' I said when I reached Ruth's office, 'just to deliver these precious goodies to your mistress.'

Peggy's sidekick on the Frankfurt stand was Lynne O'Neill, who doubled as a PA to me and David Holmes. (After Peggy's departure she took care of all Peggy's book fair duties.) Lynne was brilliant at making sure that everyone was well looked after, and she generously found ways of including any stragglers in boisterous group get-togethers. She was a big help to me – in good times and in bad. She could turn a dull day into a drama, a drama into a crisis, and a crisis into a stonking night out – and she couldn't type from my handwriting unless she had had one of those.

In the centre of the organisation, at the heart of this complex network of companies, divisions and sub-divisions, was Dot Barsby. For some crazy reason we had operated without a full-blown HR department until 1992, the year DK went public. It had been a distinctly amateurish hand-to-mouth operation, tolerable as long as the staff pay and benefits were at an acceptable level but less forgivable in cases where professional guidance was essential. Dot arrived as HR director not a minute too soon. We had known her way back in Mitchell Beazley days when she was PA to a senior director there; she had since acquired the qualifications we needed for the job. Her arrival was a breath of cheery, dauntless, practical, can-do, well-organised fresh air. She rapidly became familiar with each and every member of the burgeoning staff, and proved herself to be a highly skilled moderator between them and management. Above all, she was excellent fun and, with Carole Mackenzie, formed a partnership determined to act in the best interests of everyone. When I look back to the good times, it's the people I remember.

And what I remember about the people is their commitment. This was the glue that bound us together as a working unit and what kept so many of us so long in the service of DK and, more particularly, of one master – generally, publishing is a profession notorious for its butterfly attachments and in the course of a career it was usual to flit from one company to another. The commitment was to Peter Kindersley, for his vision and his leadership, and the values he instilled in us. One might argue that some of us stayed too long for our own good, maybe even for the good of the company if one were to look at it in purely Darwinian terms. On the other hand, when it came to the crunch of deciding whether to go or stay, the key question resided in whether anywhere else could combine fulfilment, challenge, reward and opportunity in such measure, and a company work ethic to match that which permeated every DK building. The commitment amounted to a collective positive – not always, of course, because inevitably there were grumbles and gripes, disagreements and bouts of disaffection, but what seemed unique, to me at least, was the general absence of cynicism. There was no room in the company for bruising, self-important egos. And what the commitment brought forth was the better part of ourselves – generosity of spirit, tolerance, mutual support, humour, irreverence and lasting friendships.

One of my favourite watering holes in Covent Garden is Two Brydges, a club in dedicated contrast to the glitzy self-regard of the in-places erupting across the capital. Hidden away in a Hogarthian alley, its stairs creak like doors in a Vincent Price movie, the chairs are wonky and the tables wobble, but it is comfortable and comforting. A fire burns in the grate, eclectic paintings hang on the walls, and operatic arias sluice through the rooms. It is welcoming, unpretentious, home to a ragbag of characters, mainly from the arts world, and I love it. Every year, in the week before Christmas, I would book a room for a celebratory lunch there with twenty or so of my most companionable colleagues. As the winter afternoon gave way to darkness and the legions of wine glasses glimmered in the candle light among the walnuts and the crumpled paper hats, I would reflect on what we had achieved. It might have been more books sold, or more innovative books created, but ultimately what mattered most to me was the reaffirmation of this talented group's commitment, and the privilege of their friendship.

A Lifetime of Learning

Education, education, education. This was the new Kindersley refrain and the focus of his ambition as the digital world materialised and as the spread of DKFL created a substantial sales channel. With CD-ROMs now being published online, and with a healthy proportion of teachers recruited as DKFL distributors, the opportunity was there on two fronts to bring "soft" education into the home as support for the curriculum. Peter was keen to forge close links with the educational establishment, to build a whole new business from the premise that Dorling Kindersley books and CD-ROMs were beloved of teachers and pupils alike.

It looked like a safer bet than the trade, too, which, now that the Net Book Agreement had disappeared, was becoming an aggressive battleground on price and margin. This not only threatened the stability of trade sales, it created havoc with the DKFL distributors, who never exhibited restraint when it came to complaining about obstacles in their business. And, now that email was the preferred means of communication, and they all had Peter's address, they loaded his inbox with their problems in tones that ranged from mild whingeing to full-blown hysteria. Unfortunately, unlike the conventional structure of DK as a company, where complaints could be filtered, diverted or handled by the layers of management, there was no effective barrier between Peter and the multitudes on their home computers. His reactions were variable. It sometimes meant that minority opinions loudly expressed were received with a deference that led to sweeping statements about the failure of DKFL management to implement this or that. It seemed that he could not ignore any email on his screen and the menu of complaints could be extensive, from the discovery that a children's title had been found at Costco at $6.99 while they, DKFL, were obliged to sell it at $9.99, to the more generalised bleats about the fact that some of DK's trade bestsellers were robustly illustrated sex manuals.

The first manifestation of the move towards education was the renaming of DK Family Library as DK Family Learning. At every conference Peter would stand up and make a speech justifying the change and urging all the distributors to fall in line behind his new mission statement for the company, namely to emphasise the educational benefits which our books, videos and CD-ROMs conferred. "Learning for Life" became another marketing catch phrase at this time. This change of direction created a rift among the distributors. Those who bought into it saw it as a natural evolution of what they had been selling all along, with a more specific angle to the sales pitch. The ones who didn't embrace the idea were those who were in the business for purely commercial reasons and who felt that the emphasis on educational benefits was too heavy a message to be effective. It sounded earnest rather than engaging. The DKFL management didn't seem to be totally convinced either, though they didn't make much headway if they voiced their reservations – sooner or later, they were bludgeoned into accepting the change by the immovable force of the Great Leader's diktat.

The message was spreading across the continents. In 1996 DKFL had begun operations in Russia and Australia; plans were now in place to start up in India; and openings in Germany, Mexico, Poland, Southeast Asia, Canada and South Africa were being evaluated. There were, of course, considerable cultural differences between some of these markets. In Russia, for example, a well-educated readership was hungry for substantial volumes on sophisticated subjects, though the means by which the business was locally operated was not without its risks, particularly from the powerful, well-armed elements within that society. Australia, on the other hand, was similar to the UK and US in its demand for quality books for the young, and especially for the pre-school age group. And as we expected of an Australian business, it was a typically gung-ho, go-out-and-get-them ethos, mostly dominated by vociferous women who allowed no roadblocks in their path – God help you if you were responsible for putting one there.

Having launched DKFL in that market, we decided to complete the circle in Australia and switch from packaging to publishing. Towards the end of 1996 I spent a week in a hotel on the beach at Manly interviewing candidates for the top job. This proved to be a more rewarding task than head-hunting in New York for the DK Inc CEO – most of the applicants were well known to us from our years of travelling Down Under to sell the rights to our books, and everyone seemed to take a positive attitude to the decision to become an imprint, even those companies which had most to lose from the change. In fact, it was our biggest customer that coughed up the winner. Robert Sarsfield had played a key role at Reader's Digest in pitching for DK titles for trade and catalogue sales, and sometimes for main selections. And he was a best mate to several of us who had come to know him well. So it was a tremendous boost when he agreed to leave the safe haven of RD to set up DK Publishing Pty.

Robert was an excellent hands-on manager who inspired terrific loyalty in his staff, was liked and respected by the trade, and was nimble at forging relationships with brand name institutions to lend authenticity to the Australian content of our reference books. Six months after he joined, we launched DK Publishing with a bash at the Australian Booksellers Conference in Darling Harbour. And, soon after that, the DKFL team moved in to share the publishing company's offices in North Sydney, making Australia the only country where the two businesses operated, and cooperated, in close proximity. It paid off. Both benefited from a mutual understanding of each other's priorities and modus operandi, and in typical Aussie tradition, there were no issues of snobbery or elitism to sully the atmosphere between them.

These optimistic flourishes in the southern hemisphere were

not reflected in the US, where a significant shift in the retail trade heralded difficulties for all. For some years now, DK Inc had been benefiting from the huge expansion of superstores across the country. This colonisation of the landscape by Barnes & Noble and Borders may have partially disguised any overall stagnation in the trade. The simple fact was that for every megastore they built they needed to order the inventory to fill it. By 1997 the two retailing giants had occupied just about every available prime site across the nation – frequently, it has to be said, adjacent to an existing independent which was soon forced to close its doors – and now they were reviewing their buying policy. As with W.H. Smith in the UK, the computer screen, with its bald numerical analysis of a title's rate of sale and its available stock, replaced the instincts of a good bookseller whose judgment of a book's worth was based on more subtle quantifiables than the time it spent on his shelves. The big chains then used this analysis to change

The change of name from DK Family Library to DK Family Learning reflected Peter Kindersley's vision for the business but was not universally popular with the distributors.

their pattern of ordering to "just-in-time" replenishment and at the same time substantially increase returns. Publishers, DK among them, were caught cold, and as a result our US sales for the year grew by only 3 per cent in dollar terms. But, because of the strength of sterling, this translated to a 1 per cent decline in revenue, the first year in which we had not recorded growth in that market. Multimedia was also affected by the difficulties in the US retail environment. The end-year results showed the company had stalled: turnover was marginally up, profits marginally down. It was time for reassessment.

Although DK had had one minor hiccup, in 1994, in its expansive years, a blip largely caused by third-party distribution problems, there was no indication then that the company was running out of steam. But the fact that we had hit the buffers twelve months after our best year ever was of more concern. The first reaction was to place more emphasis on marketing, hence the appointment to the board of David Holmes as Group Sales & Marketing Director. We either had to pitch our titles more effectively to the retailers, or we had to bypass the retailers and make sure we delivered content that the public really wanted. The second reaction was to shore up and expand the direct-selling operations. But that wasn't a cheap option, and while there was an abiding conviction in Peter Kindersley's mind that the future of books and CD-ROMs lay in home selling, he knew that the impetus to open DKFL in multiple markets had to be controlled and justified, and that the first priority to be tackled was the cost base on the home front.

It was a tense time. If asked to put a date on when the tide in the affairs of DK turned, I would prick the calendar in the autumn of 1997. It wasn't just that the growth had been pegged back or that we were forced to dig deep to satisfy the City analysts that better times were just around the corner (they weren't); it was a feeling that, after a heady stretch of conquest and reward, the company had turned in on itself. The blame game started, sometimes vindictively. It was no surprise, for example, that Peter Gill left to join Pearson in a senior position. He was clearly weary of abusive meetings in which Kindersley humiliated him for his "lack of vision" when what he was trying to get across were a few reality checks on DK's financial position.

There were staff redundancies, a reduction in the number of office spaces occupied (we had practically colonised the Covent Garden area), and a new policy instigated to reduce the direct staff costs on books by outsourcing as much work as possible to freelancers. The atmosphere turned fretful and peevish. And misjudgments crept in. Whereas in the past Peter had made many decisions against which people had railed, he had usually been right, at least for a percentage high enough to trust his wisdom and his instincts. Now, for whatever reason – perhaps the reality of facing up to a slowdown in the business, the difficulties presented by expanding alternative sales operations to the trade, or by his own self-doubts about how the company should be positioned before he could think about his own exit strategy – he was distracted and this seemed to impinge on his decision-making.

I had shared an office with him for the life of the company, and I could read his moods almost better than I could read my wife's. If I had a skill in that business, it was an ability to interpret his wishes to the other managers and staff, to realise that sometimes when he said yes, he actually meant no, and vice versa. We were at times very close. I remember well how he took me into his confidence when his father was dying, a time when I saw all that was compassionate and wise in that artistic vein which joined the Kindersley bloodline. If you went to Peter with a problem, he could be the sweetest person you ever met. On the other hand, if you betrayed a weakness that diminished you as a player in the company, he could be brutally pragmatic. But, contrary or not, I had become so used to his mercurial changes that I viewed both sides of him with familiar affection, and drew on my sense of humour to defuse the more acerbic outbursts. Fortunately, he seemed to enjoy my habitual irreverence and shared my penchant for ridiculing pomposity and self-importance, and thus our daily working partnership was often characterised by a jokey camaraderie. We worked co-dependently but also semi-independently. I would ask his advice about a title over which I had doubts. He would ask mine over other miscellaneous matters. Together we would review work-in-progress on books when editors and designers came into the office to request a sign-off. As a non-designer I learned everything from him about how to use both sides of the brain.

Now Peter had moved upstairs to share an office with Rod Hare. It was a logical enough move for the chairman and chief executive to be close to the group managing director, but it signalled a shift in our relationship. I was less in tune with the way his mind was working. Perhaps this was a good thing, because he started to make decisions with which I disagreed, sometimes profoundly, and would undoubtedly have quarrelled over. On the other hand, I doubt I could have persuaded him to reverse them. The most bizarre was the deal which he and Rod struck with Bertelsmann to acquire the rights to the *Chronicle* books franchise, a series that had been highly successful a decade earlier with its bulky volumes recording history day by day or year by year, written as newspaper journalism in the historic present tense. This was a brand now past its sell-by-date, but somehow they contrived to offer Bertelsmann a royalty deal that wouldn't have earned out during a Thousand-Year Reich – well, maybe a Fifty-Year version – and which left DK saddled with an annual debt that hit the bottom line for years afterwards. And it wasn't a deal on which the rest of the board was consulted, an uncomfortable foretaste of what was to follow.

Enter the Marketing Man

One might imagine that a company with the name Industrial Light and Magic would be situated somewhere in the urban sprawl of Los Angeles or Silicon Valley, in which case it would have been easier to find than it was. The Lucas Ranch is discreetly hidden away off a country road an hour or so north of San Francisco. You drive down a track bordered by gently rolling hills reminiscent of Scotland towards what looks like a Victorian hunting lodge. This building, in fact a relatively recent reproduction, houses the headquarters of LucasFilm, while tucked away at the edges of the valley various barn-like structures contain the personnel and special effects for Industrial Light and Magic, George Lucas's box of tricks factory which had earned him the devotion of millions when the *Star Wars* trilogy aired in the 1970s.

It was Neal Porter in the US office of Dorling Kindersley who alerted us to the fact that the licensing arm of LucasFilm was seeking tenders for tie-in books to the new *Star Wars* movie planned for release in the summer of 1999. After a gap of 21 years since the last film, this was reckoned to be the hottest and most anticipated event of the decade, and publishers, toy manufacturers and licensors of merchandise scrambled to get their share of the pot. This was new territory for DK, but it didn't faze us. It was self-evident that we should capitalise on the graphic design style for which we were known and use that to give us a unique and distinctive advantage in our pitch. It was helpful, too, to learn that Lucy Autrey Wilson, in whose gift the licences lay, was a fan of DK.

A small group of us, including Neal, Roger Priddy, and Fiona Macmillan, who was the children's publisher in charge of licensed projects, travelled to the ranch where we presented our case, laying out our best-selling series on the table – *Eyewitness* books, *Visual Dictionaries*, *Cross-Sections*, sticker books, etc. We had proposals for different titles and different formats. And we had a strong suit in hand with the fact that DK was now a publisher, and a brand in all the English language markets – we had recently hoisted our flag in Canada under the skilled guidance of Loraine Taylor (another former RD executive), were established in South Africa, both in the trade and through the DKFL network, and had opened an operation in India under Bikram Grewal. It meant that we could coordinate the manufacturing and the publicity campaigns for the titles, and furthermore the company now boasted an international sales force of more than 50 people who would work with LucasFilm licensors to secure publishing deals around the world.

Lucy endorsed our bid. We settled on four hardback titles

– a Visual Dictionary, and a book of Cross-Sections of the Star Wars vehicles and spaceships, one of each to cover the earlier films, and then one of each to be specifically tied to the new movie, *Episode I* – plus various sticker books. Securing the deal was one thing; making the books another. The film was still work-in-progress and subject to punitive restrictions – the editors, designers and illustrators assigned to the project were obliged to sign the equivalent of the Official Secrets Act on pain of being zapped with a lightsaber. We had to second some of them to work at the Ranch so that they could have access to the characters and hardware without the risk of secrets leaking out. For them it was probably the best fun, though not without its hazards. To photograph some of the key robotic characters which had featured in the previous films, it was necessary to reassemble them. For the most part they were in bits and pieces in cardboard boxes all over the studio floor where they had lain for twenty years. Additionally, the DK people had to be wary of George Lucas himself. It was made clear to them at the outset that he did not care for direct eye contact and that if one saw him approaching, to look the other way. One designer became so flustered when he glimpsed the great man walking in his direction, he looked the other way, as instructed, tripped and fell headlong into a carton full of C-3PO's severed limbs.

The landing of the Star Wars contracts certainly provided a boost to the Children's Division, which could anticipate putting together a budget for the following year, 1998-99, with at least two bankable bestsellers on the list, possibly four. And it opened our eyes to what else might be achieved by landing tie-in publications with other big movie franchises. It was the kind of new initiative the business needed as the year-end figures at June 1998 revealed, with turnover and profits only marginally up on the stagnant 1997 figures.

The late summer of 1998 proved to be a critical period in DK's history, so it is perhaps worth noting the statistics which Bankside Consultants Ltd (Charles Ponsonby's financial PR firm) handed out to accompany those year-end results. They give a snapshot of the state of DK's world.

1. Annually, DK sells approximately 60 million books, CD-ROMs and videos in a total of over 115 countries and almost 50 languages, and transacts business with more than 400 publishers.

2. At 30 June 1998, DK had originated over 2,400 titles – approximately 1,100 in DK Adult, 1,000 in DK Children's, 200 in DK Vision and 60 in DK Interactive Learning (as Multimedia had been renamed) – since its foundation in 1974, of which over 80 per cent are still in print.

3. In 1998, DK published approximately 320 titles, of which approximately 110 were DK Adult, 150 DK Children's, and 20 DK Interactive Learning.

4. DK Adult's average sale per title is some 210,000 copies, DK Children's more than 150,000 copies – both hugely in excess of the market norm. At least 37 titles (26 Adult, 11 Children's) have sold more than 1 million copies.

5. The bestsellers have been the *Red Cross First Aid Manual* (over 6 million copies in 22 languages); the *Family Medical Guide* (over 6 million copies in 15 languages) and the *A-Z Medical Encyclopedia* (over 5 million copies in 16 languages).

6. The *Eyewitness Guides* (100 published to date in 36 languages) have sold over 38 million copies.

7. Sales of DK books exceed 350 million copies.

8. DK Interactive Learning worldwide unit sales in the year increased by 22 per cent to 1,650,000.

9. DK has a headcount of 1,318, including approximately 230 freelancers, of which almost 600 are editors, designers, producers, animators and programmers.

10. DK Family Learning has approaching 23,000 independent distributors worldwide.

Is this a company at the peak of its powers with a commanding worldwide reach, or is this an organisation stretched to the limits of its management capabilities and pedalling hard to keep up? Was the next big leap forward just around the corner or was the search for the next great innovative idea proving as elusive as the Holy Grail? It was perhaps in the context of such questions that Peter Kindersley came to the conclusion that he needed to recruit a heavyweight to sit alongside him at the head of the company. He decided – to the approval of the City who disliked the combination of chairman and chief executive in one person – to free himself of the latter. In theory at least. Rod Hare was let go and Peter, as if donning his most imperial toga, announced to the board that he, and he alone, would interview the candidates put up for selection and when he had made his choice, the senior management could meet the heir apparent before he was officially anointed. But this was merely a courtesy, no more than that. If we had objections to his choice, we would probably just have to live with it.

The interview with the chosen one was inconclusive. There

was something fidgety and not quite settled about the guy, which erupted in a rash display of over-confidence.

'I believe I can more than double the size of this company in the next five years,' he declared. 'No problem. You have one of the best and least exploited brands in the business. All you need is marketing. I mean real marketing.'

Oh, God, one of those, I thought. But I was willing to see if this claim could be supported.

Afterwards it emerged that Peter had been faced with a choice between two candidates, one of whom he described as a 'very safe pair of hands'. ('Exactly what we need,' was one senior opinion. 'The last thing we want is a clone of PK.') But he hadn't allowed us to interview the safe alternative. Peter had seen a man who was all too ready to embrace his vision, to elaborate on it and then enlarge it to mind-boggling dimensions.

The new chief executive (whom I will call Marketing Man) seemed to inhabit a world that veered between reality and fantasy. As soon as he was installed, the balance of power within the management shifted on its axis. He shared an office with Kindersley and together the two of them built their towering cumuli of frothy ambition. Peter, for the first time in my experience, was putty in the hands of another. He gave MM free rein to do whatever he wanted. The more ambitious it was, the better Peter liked it, regardless of cost or the impact it might have on others. I began to feel sidelined. Peter no longer consulted me, and the companionable relationship we had enjoyed since the beginning of DK was at risk of dissolving, so in thrall was he to his new accomplice and so sceptical was I about the benefits this relationship might deliver. It was also clear that MM felt an antipathy toward me.

In due course Marketing Man took his knife to the senior management, carving up the sales, marketing and distribution personnel and importing a bunch of cronies from his previous business life, most of whom had zero experience of book publishing. He then informed me that in his opinion certain members of the creative management were looking 'deadbeat' and I ought to consider replacing them. I told him where he could shove that idea. He duly went and fired them himself.

The most high-profile casualty was David Houston, a hard-nosed Scot from Harper Collins who had replaced Peter Gill as CFO. David was scrupulous in his line-by-line calculations of the end-year projections, but as these apparently did not tally with what the CEO expected the company to deliver, he was summarily dismissed. In David's place, Alan Fort, recently of the Savoy, was hired. But the situation at board level deteriorated as Kindersley, Marketing Man and Fort formed a mini-cabal of their own whose mid-weekly board meetings now excluded the other directors. I complained about this to Anita Fulton (who had succeeded Giles Cunningham as legal director), but there was no response from the Gang of Three.

Marketing Man turned his attention to DKFL, Peter Kindersley's pet project. He wasn't impressed by the rate of growth, especially in the USA.

'There are too many barriers between the distributors and their customers,' he declared. 'Ordering a book and selling it should be dead simple. We need to sort it.'

Alan Luce was put under the spotlight and granted no reprieve. Peter and MM flew to the Midwest and gave him the bum's rush. Then they convened a conference of the senior distributors.

MM addressed the gathering, who were still in shock from Alan's sudden exit, and informed them of his plans to revitalise the business. There were four main points. Firstly, the distributors could obtain catalogues for free instead of having to buy them. This prompted clapping from the floor. Then he announced that he was going to let them have free books to give away with those they sold, for a period of six months, in the belief that this would really boost recruitment. A cheer from the audience. The third benefit would be an immediate increase in the marketing spend on every single title to power up the sales. Another burst of applause. And, finally, he declared that he was going to slash the cover price of every book. A huge cheer. He told them that he wanted to make DKFL the fastest growing direct-selling business in the country, and that he would do whatever it took to make that happen. They were now standing on their feet, whistling and stamping.

In theory this sounded like an excellent scheme for ramping up sales and adopting new recruits to the network but the question of its effect on the profit margins of the business was left unaddressed – at least in a main board meeting. It seemed to be a case of not worrying about that while the focus was on driving the DKFL top line revenues through the stratosphere. This was pretty much a mirror image of what was happening throughout all the business areas of DK – concentrate on building sales as the priority rather than paying attention to margins. The company was approaching £200 million in turnover; Marketing Man had set a target of reaching £500 million in five years.

If the company is still solvent in five years, I thought. At the rate he is raiding the till for his marketing sprees it will be cleaned out by then. The sales line may get to look impressive but it will all be froth on top. Nothing underneath. What was Peter thinking? It was impossible to know. He just grinned. The experience of having such a driven personality to run the business appeared to cause him endless amusement.

MM was certainly energetic. He embarked on his own world tour of the DK subsidiaries. He seemed immune to jetlag. He spent a morning in India, and a day in Australia. In every venue he made the same speech with the same PowerPoint image on the screen behind him. It was a photograph of a toy train on which cut-out pictures of the directors were superimposed. Peter and I sat on top of the engine, MM was in the driver's cab, marketing in the first coach, sales in the second, and services (finance, production, distribution) in the guard's van.

'The point about DK is this,' he would say, indicating the train with a stick. 'It is a creatively led company, which is why Peter and Christopher are at the front, backed by marketing, which drives the sales, and supported by the service operations, and it's my business to keep the train moving along the tracks. And I'll tell you this for free, this train will be two or three times bigger in five years time, and every single division, subdivision and subsidiary company is going to have to grow proportionately. If they don't, they'll be hearing from me.'

He toured the creative teams in Covent Garden and expounded the same message.

'I'll tell you this for free. There's nothing wrong with this company that brilliant marketing won't put right. Don't worry about anything except continuing to produce fantastic books. I'll be responsible for seeing they get the marketing they deserve, and I'll be responsible for ensuring they are sold. In big numbers. Very big numbers, as long as the marketing is properly targeted.'

'Why does he always say "I'll tell you this for free"?' asked one of my senior colleagues when I took them to lunch.

'Because it is the only thing he says which actually is free. Everything else is going to cost a fortune, believe me.'

'God help us,' sighed another. 'Do you think he knows what he's doing? Sounds to me like he's driving the company straight off a cliff.'

'I expect he won a gold medal in the luge,' said a third. 'He obviously knows how to go downhill very fast.'

'Without brakes. That's what it feels like.'

'Looks more like a two man bobsleigh to me,' said another. 'Peter's sitting behind him, digging him in the ribs and telling him to go faster.'

'Aren't the rest of the board worried by all this?' I was asked. 'Don't we need some checks and balances in place?'

'Yeah, but I've got to tell you,' I said, 'the board, in its everyday working capacity, has been cut down to three people – Kindersley, Marketing Man and Fort. They are determining the way forward. The main board meetings are now just for routine reporting. The rest of us no longer seem to have an influence. I have protested but it has been ignored. It's no joke. Watch this space.'

'But can't you have a private word with Peter? After all, you have worked alongside him for so long. Surely he will listen to you?'

Peter Kindersley rides through Delhi en route to opening the
newly built offices of DK India, the last jewel in the company crown.

'I have tried,' I replied. 'I even wrote him a personal letter to his home address. He didn't even acknowledge it. He's undergone a dramatic change. In the old days you could rely on his decision-making. Even if you thought it was crazy at the time, in the end, more often than not, he was proved right. Now that instinct seems to have deserted him. The presence of MM seems to have flipped a switch inside him, and now most of his decisions are questionable at best.'

'Why do you think Peter's behaviour has changed so dramatically? It can't just be the influence of MM.'

'No,' I replied. 'I've thought about it a lot. I reckon it's to do with his uncertainty about the long-term future of the company, i.e. when he retires. In business schools they call it Founder's Syndrome, the dilemma of knowing that at some point you have to let go of what you have created but cannot decide in whose hands you will entrust its future. His children aren't going to take it on. So he's placed all his chips on this appointment. It's like gambling your life savings on a single number at roulette.'

'Do you think he's secretly worried by that?'

'Maybe. It's difficult to be sure because he has become so hard to reach. He reminds me of King Lear at the division of his kingdom. Those who were loyal and loved him most were cast aside or exiled.'

'God, that sounds ominous.'

Bring on the Men in White Coats

The *Star Wars* books featuring the original films were published for the Christmas market in 1998, a couple of months after Marketing Man joined the company. While it was reckoned that there could be pretty healthy sales for all those fans who harboured memories of the earlier trilogy, it was estimated that the real feeding frenzy would peak when the new movie premiered the following spring and we published the tie-in titles. For MM the opportunity was irresistible. He saw *Star Wars* as the ideal vehicle for making his indelible mark on the fortunes of Dorling Kindersley and proving to the world that he was the man who could ramp up the sales of a bestseller like no other.

'Whatever number you put down in the sales forecast,' he announced, 'I'll bet I can double it, maybe even quadruple it. No other publisher could make these books like DK, and no other publisher has our global reach. We are going to sell millions.'

Each of the publishing territories – UK, US, Australia, Canada – submitted their estimates. They totalled five million copies, a pretty remarkable quantity for a relatively slim sales window. MM wasn't satisfied. He announced that from now on he would assume sole charge of the *Star Wars* project and that the marketing and production departments would report exclusively to him. In other words, he would control the promotional and publicity spend and he would control the print orders.

This unilateral approach was alarming. I had already experienced the negative effects of it after he had elected to visit John Roberts, then the senior executive on the books side of BCA, and demand that their book club deals no longer be exclusive. John had terminated the meeting and ordered his colleagues to cancel the purchase of a number of key DK titles, including a *World History Atlas* that we were about to launch and which we had been developing for some years in the hope that it would become a main selection for the book club. This was a major blow. We were BCA's biggest account. A mutually beneficial relationship, carefully nurtured over twenty years, was in the can. I turned to Peter for support, but his response was tepid, and in any event the damage had been done.

In the spring of 1999, DK's 25th anniversary year, it was decided to hold a mega sales conference for all the sales and marketing territories in Orlando, Florida. No expense was spared. The cast list was huge, and included both trade and DKFL representatives from the UK, US, Canada, Australia, South Africa, and India (where DK was now active on both fronts); from France, where DK had started its own children's imprint under Steve Bateman; from Germany, where we were about to become full-scale publishers under Daniel Bruecher; the directors and managers from international sales; and the leading players on the creative side responsible for books, CD-ROMs and videos. With the warm sun on our backs and the promise of a bumper year coming up, it was a chance to loosen the pucker strings and have an all-round good time. Few failed to seize the opportunity. Late at night and into the small hours, the hot tub by the swimming pool swarmed with bodies as they frolicked under the stars. Wine glasses and cigarette stubs lay scattered on the grass. All the scene lacked to mimic the last days of Rome's gilded empire were a few bunches of grapes, peeled and dropped into our mouths by nubile handmaidens or lissom catamites.

Inside the conference room the following day, the mood was rather different. Peter Kindersley, predictably, had not indulged in the evening wassail but his mood was still akin to a bear with a sore head.

'You people have got to change,' he announced from the stage without any preamble or context. 'You've got to realise that if you don't change, this company doesn't have a future.'

Nobody knew what he was talking about. Change how? And why? He wasn't congratulating us on past achievements or exhorting us to greater heights, as one might expect on such an occasion; he was accusing us. What had we done?

'The world is changing faster than you know,' he continued. 'And unless we adapt with it, we will be lost.'

So it went on. Heads drooped. It was a depressing speech, more a statement of his own confusion than anything else.

Marketing Man stepped into the breach, determined to lift the mood. But what we got was the bloody toy train PowerPoint once again, which everyone in the room had seen at least once.

'Now I'm showing you this analogy of the train again,' he said, 'because I want to emphasise how important it is in relation to achieving our target sales on the biggest project this company has undertaken. Marketing supports creative to drive sales. In this case, humungous marketing and humungous sales.'

Then he got down to the brass tacks of the campaign to boost *Star Wars*, which was followed by a listing on the screen of the group sales estimates, showing the breakdown by territory.

'Let's look at these one by one,' he said. 'First, the US. Danny anticipates selling three million copies. Well, he doesn't know it yet but I've got news for him; I'm going to double that right now to six million. And that's for starters….'

It continued in this vein. In each country the numbers were ratcheted up way beyond the carefully worked out local projections. There were mild protestations, but these were batted away. In the heady euphoria of a sales conference in Florida, perhaps people were ready to believe Peter Kindersley had hired a miracle worker, that he knew whereof he spoke, and that we would indeed outsell our expectations. But did anyone in the room that day feel the first prickling of a breeze on their neck? Did they hear that faint rustling of the leaves in the treetops when the air becomes quiet and heavy in the vacuum before a storm?

An unlikely pairing. Peter Kindersley clasps a display model of R2-D2, one of many marketing devices created to drive the sales of the *Star Wars* titles.

These titles, imaginatively created in collaboration with LucasFilm, were highly successful. Unfortunately they became indelibly linked to the demise of DK as an independent company.

The *Star Wars* books were launched in May at a lavish Hollywood-style bash in Los Angeles, and the sales volumes in the first month gave a welcome boost to our year-end figures in June. Total company revenues were just shy of £200 million, and profits up to £11.5 million (before taking into account a net loss on the closure of the DK Russian operation). The publishing markets had done well, and we were about to switch from licensing to publishing in two foreign language territories – France and Germany. DK Interactive Learning was having a tougher time on the sales front with its enforced switch to more overtly educational titles, and DK Vision wasn't reporting growth. But, thanks to the massive marketing push in DKFL, the number of distributors worldwide had risen to 30,000. It seemed that the business might now be really poised for liftoff, especially in the US.

They are not long, the days of wine and roses. When I returned from a holiday in France in mid-August, expecting as usual to be involved in the preparation of the year-end results presentations, I discovered that the format had been changed.

'It won't be a collective presentation this year,' Peter informed me.

I asked what had prompted that. Peter was evasive. Over the next couple of weeks he would neither speak to me unless I addressed him directly, nor would he look me in the eye. He started to assume control of ideas I was proposing to the creative teams. Eventually I asked him for clarification.

'I've spent a lot of time discussing this with MM,' he said. 'We have decided that I should take exclusive control of the creative side while he assumes complete control of the business aspects. I'm therefore going to ask you to take early retirement at Christmas.'

It was hard to swallow. We had a long-standing mutual agreement that we could both choose the moment when we wanted to retire. A quarter of a century since the small band of us had risked all by following him to set up the company, since the day when he had driven us through London and turned to face us in the back of his VW camper van as he weaved through the traffic, saying 'Trust me, trust me, trust me!' with all the intensity of a preacher man, he had broken that bond.

'What about Linda?' I asked.

'Yes, her too,' he said, quick to kill two birds with one stone.

Two days later, on September 2nd, a fire (the third in DK's history) spread across the roofs from Earlham Street to Shelton Street and destroyed the top half of the building, which housed a section of the Adult creative division plus the picture library containing some two million images. Luckily most of the images in their fireproof cabinets escaped unscathed. But there was something ominous about the event. It was 333 years to the day since the Great Fire of London. Was the Devil at work?

He certainly seemed to have a hand in the manner and timing of my departure announcement. September 15th had long been blocked out as the day on which DK would formally celebrate its 25th anniversary. A lavish black-tie dinner/dance at the Savoy was planned – no expense spared (natch, in the Marketing Man era). There would be 25 tables, each one dedicated to the theme of a DK title, and all the great and the good from our stable of authors, artists, agents and institutional partners, along with the senior staff, would be present. It was a given that at the end of the dinner Peter Kindersley would make a speech celebrating our successes and reiterating his lofty ideals; it was likewise expected that I would follow him with a more light-hearted rehearsal of the company's history.

The board concluded that to announce my "retirement" before the day of the dinner would be inappropriate as it could affect the mood of the evening. Peter therefore proposed that I announce it myself at the conclusion of my speech. I was being asked to play the Fool at the King's behest, to mimic joy while hiding pain behind a mask of mirth. The first draft of my speech had revolved around the 25 good things about Dorling Kindersley; now I needed to revise it, because there were 26 items to include. I reconstructed it as an A-Z, most of which constituted, even if expressed in mildly irreverent humour, paeans of praise for our Great Leader. When I came

to deliver it on the night, I hoped that the cumulative effects of food, wine and too much oratory had numbed my audience's senses by the time I reached Z for Zeitgeist. This was the cue to declare that Linda and I were now ageing lions ready to seek the shadows of the long grass, making way for younger lions to have their days in the sun – an escapist metaphor to disguise a lie. I knew at once that the timing was wrong, that it was an intrusively downbeat moment. But before I could assess the reaction the Abba tribute band came to my rescue, and as they struck up "Dancing Queen" I threw myself onto the dance floor.

Later I felt the empty post-performance exhaustion of an actor. Looking back I do not remember much about the speech. What I recall is the sea of faces gazing up at the podium, lit by smiles on a late summer night. They were happy, they felt secure, the future of their publishing fortunes was full of bright promise. The captain had assured them they were on a well-nigh unsinkable ship, and that the first officer now on the bridge would give them safe passage through the ice floes. They had everything to celebrate and nothing to fear. And the band played on…

My final duty was a round-the-world farewell trip, firstly to Australia where they were holding their own 25th anniversary tribute. Afterwards I had a heart-to-heart with Robert Sarsfield.

'I've got to tell you – I'm faced by a real problem here, mate,' he said.

'What is it?'

'*Star Wars*,' he replied.

'What about it?'

'I'm at the end of my tether. We put in our forecast that we would sell 125,000 copies, tops. Did our chief executive accept that? Did he hell! First up, he forces me to order twice that for this market, and now, without any reference to me, I discover he has sanctioned yet another printing of 250,000 copies, and what's more, they're already on a boat – destination Australia! What am I supposed to do – feed them to the ruddy sheep?'

This was incredible. Nobody had ever sold in such numbers, not even Bryce Courtenay, the country's best-selling author. The question was, who knew about it?

I flew to the US for the Fall sales conference, held in

Peter and Juliet Kindersley cut the ribbon to open the newly commissioned warehouse in Nashville. Ironically it did not have enough capacity for the Star Wars titles.

Nashville that year so that we could at the same time witness the ceremonial opening of the brand new warehouse which Marketing Man had commissioned. After a brief tour of the facility, we stood outside and waited for Peter and Juliet to cut the ceremonial ribbon. But I was puzzled. There were no *Star Wars* books on the shelves.

'Why aren't they there?' I asked Andrew Berkhut, who, as the Children's VP at DK Inc, knew more about the numbers than anyone else.

'Shh!' he whispered.

'Why shh?' I replied.

'Because there are too many of them to fit in."

'Too many? How many have you got?'

'Thirteen million.'

'You're kidding me.'

'I'm not.'

'Holy shit! How on earth did that happen?'

'We kept getting phone calls from MM, demanding that we order more copies. We told him that we had more than enough, but he wouldn't let it rest. "Just print the fucking things!" he would shout. "Just print the fucking things! This is going to be bigger than the Bible!" I thought he was drunk, but he wasn't.'

I couldn't believe what I was hearing.

I sought out the heads of the other territories. Peter Stafford, the UK MD, told me he had at least twice as many copies as he could sell in a lifetime. Others relayed similar tales of their bulging inventory.

I totted up the numbers. Eighteen million copies printed.

Estimated sales: five million. Thirteen million overstocks. Bring on the men in white coats.

Back in London, the last Holding Board meeting I would attend as a director of DK was scheduled for late November. When the draft agenda was circulated there was no item relating to *Star Wars*. I called Anita Fulton, who combined the role of company secretary with that of legal director, and requested that the inventory issue be added. She said she would raise the point with Peter and MM. But when the final agenda arrived on my desk it was not there. I would have to introduce it at the end of the meeting under Any Other Business.

'I have to raise this matter,' I began when my turn came, 'because it has been, in my view, and in spite of my request to have it included, deliberately omitted from the agenda. You can correct me if I have got the figures wrong, but my research concludes that we have so far printed eighteen million copies of the *Star Wars* titles. At the same time the markets are reiterating that they do not anticipate selling significantly more copies than they had originally budgeted before the Florida conference. In other words, five million copies. That will leave us with thirteen million books stuffed in warehouses around the world. Just how exactly are these copies going to be disposed of?'

Marketing Man was cornered but, true to form, he responded with his customary bluster.

'You don't know about it because you don't need to worry about it. We are going to sell many more copies than the markets claim. And I have an arrangement in place if there are overstocks.'

'What sort of arrangement?' I asked. 'You can't remainder thirteen million books. In any event, our contract with LucasFilm categorically prohibits us from remaindering the titles or selling them off at promotional prices. And furthermore I do need to know about it. As deputy chairman, I would find myself directly responsible if Peter had the misfortune to fall under a bus tomorrow and I'm not about to sacrifice my house, my family and my worldly goods if this company goes under on the back of fatuous decisions on print runs which you deliberately concealed – from me, at least. Nor am I prepared to be detained at Her Majesty's pleasure. Are you?'

Marketing Man ignored this. Peter Kindersley said nothing. He seemed strangely detached from the whole business. A little smile still played about his lips as though he was finding this confrontational situation an amusing sideshow.

'Presumably you have considered how the auditors will react to thirteen million copies of unsold stock in our warehouses?' I continued. 'Do you honestly believe they will allow you to carry those forward on the books when we haven't a hope in hell of selling them?'

'Yes, we have thought about it,' said MM. 'And, yes, I believe they will allow it.'

'This is absolutely incredible!' I said.

The rest of the board were speechless. I began to wonder if I was going mad. Perhaps they just saw my outburst as the last gasps of a Dead Man Walking.

The meeting broke up. Juliet Kindersley and Robin

Holland-Martin, both non-executive directors, followed me into my office.

'This company is heading for the rocks,' I said. 'You'd better wake up to it.'

I was trembling with anger.

'You don't understand, Christopher,' said Peter after Juliet had reported back to him. 'MM has got everything under control. He's done a deal with a media credits company. We won't have to worry about overstocks.'

'A media credits company? What does that mean?'

'It's complicated to explain …'

'I'll bet it is.'

He didn't respond.

'Peter,' I said in a resigned way, 'it pains me to say this after all the years we have worked together, but in my opinion you have been completely misled. This company is headed in the wrong direction. It could be catastrophic. I can't believe that no one else on the board can see it. Or if they can see it, why do they say nothing and do nothing?'

I walked out of the room and left the building. It seemed like a final act. I crossed the Piazza, head bowed, hands thrust into my jacket pockets. A thin rain was falling. The cobbles grew slick underfoot. How did this come to be? I thought. One spends years in a communal collective with the highest aspirations, working to build a company from the ground up. It grows to be recognised around the world for its style and its quality. Everyone who works there is proud to be part of the enterprise. Then along comes a maverick with his own agenda and dynamites it in a matter of months.

I raised my arms and shouted at the weeping sky: '"We cry that we are come to this great stage of fools,"' to the consternation of a tramp who was sheltering in a doorway. I gave him a handful of coins.

'King Lear,' I said. 'I expect you know the feeling well enough.'

I turned on my mobile and called Jackie Douglas.

'Jackie, I need to talk. It's important. Can you round up the usual suspects – David, Andrew, Daphne, Robin, Michael, Stuart, Alan – you know, any companion spirits who are free – and meet me in Two Brydges? Lunch is on me. Or rather the Albanian Book Club.'

'The Albanian Book Club? What's that?'

'It's what I put on my expenses when I think the company should pay for a staff lunch. I suppose there's a chance some weevil in the Inland Revenue will query it one day, but, frankly, my dear, I don't give a damn.'

'Christopher, have you been drinking?'

'Not yet. Not yet. But believe me, the day is young….'

Over an extended lunch, I kept my fears about the future of the company to myself, but inevitably the conversation turned to the issue of the *Star Wars* printings.

'I can't get my head round this,' said one of the group. 'How much did Peter know about the printings, and, if he knew, why didn't he stop it?'

'He assures me that he had no knowledge of the scale of the reprints,' I said. 'But there must have been some people who knew, apart from the CEO and the production director. Who can say where the truth lies? In any event, as far as my own position is concerned, I was kept in the dark and that is unforgivable. If the company should run into difficulties, ignorance is no defence. It's completely unacceptable to me that this situation has been allowed to develop.'

My feelings were so conflicted. I owed Peter everything – he had made me, and many of my colleagues, independently wealthy, and I had experienced a working life with him of such exhilaration, unpredictability, and, above all, thrilling fulfilment that I wouldn't have exchanged it for 'a wilderness of monkeys'. I could have shrugged and walked away to a deckchair in the sun. But the attachment I had to the company was visceral. And to see it so wantonly brought low lit a fuse within me that I couldn't extinguish.

I left at Christmas. Three weeks into the new millennium my prophecy was fulfilled. In early January Marketing Man had toured the City institutions, brazenly talking up the company's prospects. The shares soared to an all-time high. A week or so later the guillotine had fallen. The auditors confronted Peter Kindersley with the unambiguous truth. Marketing Man was shown the door. The newspapers had a field day with endless punning on the theme of Darth Vader and the force deserting DK: '*Star Wars* a Horror for DK' (*Evening Standard*); '£25m in Black Hole after *Star Wars* Flop' (*The Guardian*); 'Phantom Menace Hits Dorling Kindersley' (*The Independent*). The latter went on to refer to Marketing Man's leadership as 'more Del Boy Trotter than Jedi Warrior'. The share price went into freefall and Peter announced the company was for sale. As an increased lending facility from the bank had been agreed but not actually formalised

guardian.co.uk

News   Sport   Comment   Culture   Business   Money   Life & style

Culture › Books

£25m in black hole after Star Wars flop

Lisa Buckingham, city editor
The Guardian, Tuesday 25 January 2000 1(...)
Article history

The force deserted the children's book
yesterday as the group revealed that i(...)
massively over-ordering Star Wars bo(...)

The company's chief executive, Jame(...)
the chairman and 30% shareholder, P(...)

THE INDEPENDENT   BOOKS

News   Opinion   Environment   Sport   Life & Style   **Arts & Entertainment**   Tra

Art ˅   Architecture   Music ˅   Classical ˅   Films ˅   TV & Radio ˅   Theatre & Dance ˅   Comedy ˅   Boo

Home › Arts & Entertainment › Books › News

'Star Wars' failure leaves black hole where publisher's profits used to be

By Jojo Moyes

Tuesday, 25 January 2000   ˅ SHARE   🖶 PRINT ARTICLE   ✉ EMAIL ARTICLE   ˄ A TEXT SIZE

It was the most-hyped film in history; the long-awaited prequel to an intergalactic battle waged over
[...]indersley became the unlikeliest victim of

[...]equel to an intergalactic battle waged over
[...]indersley became the unlikeliest victim of

[...]ks and merchandise left the children's and
[...]es of £25m in the six months leading up to

[...]a "hair shirt" statement, he revealed that
[...]rced to make a provision for £14m worth of
[...]om Menace failed to meet expectations.

[...]onths up to 31 December, but sold just three
[...]d, amounted to some £18m.

HOME PAGE   TODAY'S PAPER   VIDEO   MOST POPULAR   TIMES TOPICS

The New York Times

Business

WORLD   U.S.   N.Y. / REGION   BUSINESS   TECHNOLOGY   SCIENCE   HEALTH   SPORTS   OP(...)

Pearson Will Buy Dorling Kindersley In $496 Million Deal

Published: Monday, April (...)

Pearson P.L.C., the world's largest educational publisher, agreed on
Friday to buy Dorling Kindersley Holdings for $:311 million, or $496
million, in cash to gain multimedia titles like the Children's
Illustrated Encyclopedia and the Garde(...)

SIGN IN TO E-MA(...)
🖶 PRINT
REPRINTS

Pearson will pay 430 pence for each Do(...)
percent more than its closing price on T(...)
higher than the price on Jan. 25, the da(...)
said it was considering possible offers.

The 26-year-old Dorling Kindersley sta(...)
sales of "Star Wars" books resulted in a(...)
owns Penguin Books, The Financial Tir(...)
distribution power needed to build Dor(...)
analysts said.

BBC HOMEPAGE | WORLD SERVICE | EDUCATION   low graphics version | feedback | help

BBC NEWS

You are in: Business
Front Page   Friday, 31 March, 2000, 08:12 GMT 09:12 UK
World
UK   # Pearson buys Dorling
UK Politics   Kindersley
Business
Market Data
Economy
Companies
E-Commerce
Your Money
Business
Basics
Sci/Tech
Health
Education
Entertainment
Talking Point   The lack of demand for Star Wars book hit DK hard
In Depth
AudioVideo   International media group Pearson has bought
British publisher Dorling Kindersley (DK) for
£311m.

DK was hit in 1999 by its decision to invest
heavily in Star Wars books, which didn't sell as
well as expected.

DK is famous for its pop-up and educational
books and CD-ROMs and Pearson expects to
save money by combining it with its Penguin
books division.

Pearson is offering 430 pence per DK share.

Search BBC News Online
[   ] GO
Advanced search options

Launch console
for latest audio/video

◄ BBC RADIO NEWS
◄ BBC ONE TV NEWS
◄ WORLD NEWS
  SUMMARY
◄ BBC NEWS 24 BULLETIN
▶ PROGRAMMES GUIDE

See also:
▶ 24 Jan 00 | Business
  Star Wars book flop hits
  DK

Internet links:
▶ Pearson
▶ Dorling Kindersley

The BBC is not responsible for
the content of external
internet sites

**Links to other Business
stories are at the foot of
the page.**

– yet another madness – there was, predictably, no cash to spare. Alan Fort and Barry Roberts, the production director, struggled to buy time from printers, now nervous about bills approaching £30 million. There was no money to invest in new books. The staff, shattered, demoralised and disbelieving, were reduced to sharing tea bags. The company survived on a day-to-day basis with the banks monitoring every penny spent.

Of all the suitors, and there were initially several, Pearson was the most persistent and, with its own shares riding high in the dot com bubble, the most willing to pay close to the asking price. Eventually Peter succumbed to their overtures. The deal propelled him into the ranks of the super-rich.

A few weeks later, when the takeover was complete, half of the 1,500 employees were made redundant. The old board was dissolved. Peter and Juliet, their attention already focused on the challenges of running their organic farm, departed to the countryside. Marketing Man, to the disgust of the remaining staff, negotiated a pay off. The CV on his website subsequently boasted that he had tripled the value of Dorling Kindersley. Whatever the merits of that claim, it omits one crucial factor: the cost of achieving such growth. In fact, the company was crippled. The marketing spend for the year was revealed to have been 27 per cent of revenues; as suspected, the initiative to bolster DKFL's sales had completely eroded its profit margins. It was now a business haemorrhaging cash, and had to be closed down, causing near riots from furious distributors on four continents. In India Pathan warriors, whose wives were building a business through DKFL, threatened to come down from the hills and hold Bikram Grewal hostage. Pearson, without realising that £75 million in debts were hidden beneath the carpet, had arrived in the nick of time. There were no other suitors still in play. It was estimated later that DK would have ceased trading within a month.

As for me, I was generously summoned out of exile by Anthony Forbes Watson, CEO of Penguin UK, to resume my role as publisher and to act as a bridge between one world and the next.

After only four months' absence I was shocked by what confronted me. Not only was the scale of the debts a devastating revelation to me, but also the whole interior fabric of the company seemed to be in tatters. Management systems were in disrepair. The future publishing programme was threadbare. And a staff whose octane levels of confidence used to soar off the chart now resembled a band of shuffling refugees as they waited to hear whether they would find a home in the integrated set-up. It was akin to rebuilding a house after a bomb blast.

Meanwhile, out there in the wide world, where Peter's vision of benevolent domination through the power of our books, videos and CD-ROMs had kindled our imaginations and harnessed our energies, a strip of the landscape was undergoing an unwelcome transformation. Somewhere on the coastline of America, at the rough margins where the Atlantic brushes up against the edge of the continent, new islands of landfill were appearing, the burial grounds of millions of *Star Wars* books. Gannets, gulls and cormorants wheeled overhead and squawked as they battled for purchase on these new nesting sites. The last monument to DK's quarter century of independent life was a mountain of guano.

Epilogue

I sometimes speculate on what would have happened to Dorling Kindersley if it hadn't been torpedoed by the *Star Wars* fiasco. Would it have become a player in the world of online information? Would it have evolved into a more overtly educational business? Would DKFL have become its principal selling arm? Or would the company have subsided beneath the weight of its own baggy expansion? Certainly DK Inc was revealed as a loss-making concern after the takeover – the Marketing Man bacillus of overprinting in pursuit of optimistic top-line sales had infected a high proportion of the US titles. But maybe, as the world of publishing changed and moved on, DK might have had to accept that its best years in the sun were already behind it, that it had been a unique company at a unique time, and that time would not come again. This realisation gave me the impetus to attempt this unofficial history.

It is not the same company now. Within Pearson's corporate

maw, Multimedia disappeared along with CD-ROMs, DK Vision evaporated in a loss-making Penguin TV venture, and the trade publishing operations in the UK, US, Australia, South Africa, and India were subsumed beneath the local Penguin umbrellas. Our battle to keep DK alive as a separate imprint has effectively been lost. Of all the company's original core competences, only the international sales business has been left untouched. It remains the world leader in the field.

It took three years to bring DK back into profit. The company had to be slimmed even further, in part to counter the overheads incurred by occupying Pearson's expensive headquarters in the Strand. This building, though well-appointed, is reminiscent of a bank. Editors and designers sit at fixed stations on the huge open plan floors, staring at computer terminals. There is no creative mess. The air is as neutral as the cabin of an aeroplane. There are fine views of the river, but many refugees from Henrietta Street would have been just as happy working at trestle tables in a shed, especially if it meant freedom from the corporate shackles of bureaucracy. Too many people sit in on too many meetings, and too many books are prey to the nemesis of publishing by committee. More time is spent fiddling with numbers to make the P&L on a title work than on refining the unique virtues of the concept. As a result, less money is spent on the page than before – less even than by some of DK's competitors, in certain cases – and it shows. Publishers, as everywhere these days, kowtow to the self-styled omniscience of marketing people, while sales people kowtow to the retailers, who cut the price and shred the margin.

For all that, DK is still a powerhouse of illustrated reference publishing around the world, and I don't doubt that the long shadow cast by Peter Kindersley propels the makers of its books to reach new heights and seek out ever more innovative ways of delivering information. Whatever the lunacies of DK's last year of independent life, Peter had been the architect of the company's ascent and the touchstone of its creative excellence. And, from my intermittent re-connections with him since his departure, I know that, deep inside, he carries a burden of grief, as if for a lost child.

Acknowledgments

I count myself fortunate that my circle of family and friends is well seeded with writers, critics, designers, and clear-sighted editors. Without doubt I have benefited from their input. I therefore owe special thanks to Linda, Ben, Felicity Bryan, Michael Devenish, Jackie Douglas, Sybil del Strother, Dot Barsby, Caz Buckingham, Jinny Johnson, who also copy edited the manuscript, and Alan Buckingham, who additionally provided archive material and doubled as a photographer. I owe him a case of the finest.

I was delighted when Emma and Tom Forge agreed to design the book – for me, at least, this was a very happy experience.

I am indebted to Richard Carman, who graciously allowed me to reproduce his handsome watercolour of 9 Henrietta Street. My thanks also to Helena Peacock, Hermione Ireland, Douglas Amrine, Mary Holman and Anita Fulton for helpful research or advice; to Fergus Muir, Claire Bowers and Paul Turner at the DK Picture Library; and to Roger Field for his wise counsel.

Finally, a number of people nudged or corrected my memory of particular events or offered new insights and anecdotes (not all of which I could incorporate), but I am grateful to Christine Baker, Phil Wilkinson, Antony Melville, Jacky Spigel, Simonne Waud, and Peter Kindersley himself.

Christopher Davis

Image Credits

The author would like to thank the following for permission to reproduce their images:
Alan Buckingham: p.286; author photo on back flap.
Richard Carman: p.6.
©iStockphoto.com/djgunner: SLR Camera on Jacket; /Bluestocking: Fanned book on Jacket.
www.flickr.com/photos/dk-flickr: pp.15; 26; 57; 261; 297. (Photographers unknown).

All other images © Dorling Kindersley.
For further information see www.dkimages.com